FORWARD

2022 NATIONAL SOCIETY OF NEWSPAPER COLUMNISTS ANNUAL CONFERENCE

DRAFT 2 DIGITAL.

CONTENTS

WELCOME TO BIRMINGHAM!

BY TONY NORMAN

Tony Norman, NSNC President, 2020-2022

SOMETIMES IT FEELS like pandemic brain fog playing with our sense of time, but this time our brains and the facts are totally aligned. It has been two years since we've come together in one place under the banner of the NSNC, so we're grateful to be here in Birmingham, Alabama.

It was 2019 when we last gathered. It was in Buffalo, NY, a city many of us probably wouldn't have visited without the incentive of a good time with other columnists and opinion writers.

Buffalo was my first NSNC conference in a decade. After getting an invitation to attend, I realized I missed these annual gatherings. I wanted to reconnect with old friends and meet new colleagues who would remind me how privileged we are to be columnists and opinion writers in these times.

Covid and a litany of protocols designed to keep us all safe put the kibosh on in-person conferences in 2020 and 2021. During those lost years, I served as both vice president and president, thus cementing my return to the NSNC for the foreseeable future.

The success of these conferences is a result of the programming, the speaker lineup, the awards dinner, the recognition of outstanding work by our peers, the quality of the hospitality suite and the fun to be had during local tours.

This still leaves room for the kind of serendipity we all look forward to experiencing: polite rapport with a stranger when dinner begins only to see a budding friendship by the time the meal is over. Even introverts feel comfortable at these conferences.

So, here we are gathered once again to celebrate the art and science of column writing. This time the setting is Birmingham, a city those of us who have never been here before have heard so many good things about — or else we wouldn't be here.

Thanks for your hospitality, Birmingham. We're looking forward to the memories.

TONY NORMAN IS *an award winning journalist and columnist with the Pittsburgh Post-Gazette. Read his columns: https://www.post-gazette.com/opinion/tony-norman*

Stay in touch! Email: tonynormanwriter@gmail.com

DRAFT 2 DIGITAL®

DRAFT2DIGITAL—TAKE CONTROL OF YOUR PUBLISHING CAREER

D2D REMOVES the friction from writing and publishing, and empowers you to get your writing in front of the readers who want it most—for free. Find out more here: http://d2d.tips/conference

2022 NSNC CONFERENCE SCHEDULE

Thursday, June 9, 2022 - Doubletree by Hilton Birmingham Perimeter Park, AL

8:00 p.m. Hospitality Suite Opens. Cypress Room, 8th Floor Registration materials will be available for pickup. Go to dinner on your own, and later meet new and old friends in the Hospitality Suite. Note: On Friday and Saturday, the Hospitality Suite will be open right after the NSNC dinners to enjoy snacks, beverages, and incomparable company).

Friday, June 10, 2022

Breakfast: Registered NSNC hotel guests will enjoy a free hotel breakfast buffet in the lobby restaurant, as part of the NSNC hotel room package. M-F: 6-9 a.m., S-S: 6:30-10 a.m.
For non-hotel guests, there will be a coffee station and light refreshments at 8:00 near the general meeting rooms: Magnolia 2, 3 and 4.

8:30 a.m. – Welcome remarks, NSNC President Tony Norman

8:45 - 9:30 a.m. How to Write Columns Readers and Editors Both Want
Bonnie Jean Feldkamp

Bonnie Jean Feldkamp is both a syndicated columnist for Creators as well as the opinion editor for The Louisville Courier Journal, a Gannett publication part of the USA Today Network. She has the insider's view from both sides. Bonnie shares insights about industry trends for all things column-writing. What's new, what's changing and what both opinion editors and subscribers want to read. This session will help both staff columnists and freelance writers shape their pitches and what they write with an eye on where column-writing in the newspaper industry is headed.

9:30 - 10:15 a.m. – Your Dream Project: From Idea to Reality
Meredith Cummings

Do you have a dream project that seems out of reach? So did Meredith Cummings. This session will take you from your project dream to finding funding and making it happen.When Meredith Cummings took her old Volvo wagon, Ruby, on a 10,000-mile trip to newsrooms around the country she stepped out of her own newsroom experiences and held up a mirror to the journalists who bring us the news every day. "Who," she asked, "is watching the gatekeepers?" She visited news outlets big and small, for-profit and nonprofit, traditional and cutting-edge across all media during her #followmylede journey, writing as she went. She will talk about the behind-the-scenes work that went into her journey and what you can take from it. She will also approach a difficult issue she encountered again and again as she wrote: when to filter vs. overshare.

10:15 - 10:30 a.m. – Coffee Break

10:30 - 11:15 a.m. – The Business of Writing
Lori Duff

Licenses? Contracts? Accounting? Estate planning? What does any of that have to do with the art of writing? A lot! (Or maybe everything.) Judge Lori B. Duff will explain what you need to know to keep your writing business (yes, your writing is a business!) on the right side of the law. From navigating contract legalese, deciding whether or not to incorporate, managing business expenses, even considering what happens to your work after you're gone, Judge Duff will educate in an entertaining, understandable way. There's a reason she was awarded the title of "Atlanta's Funniest Lawyer" in 2018.

11:15 - Noon - TikTok And Reels For Writers
Rebecca Regnier

Author and columnist Rebecca Regnier turned an old column into a viral video on TikTok and opened up a whole new avenue for her work. As of January 2022, she had 25K followers and 400,000 likes. Her most viral video garnered 3.5 million TikTok views, while another had 1.5 million Facebook views. Attendees will learn how to use small snippets from columns to go viral and connect with new readers. They'll be introduced to other creators who used the platforms to snag book deals. Discover the world of BookTok and AuthorTok where readers and writers are connecting.

Noon to 1:30 p.m. – Lunch & Keynote held in Daffodil Foyer
John Archibald, Pulitzer Prize-winning journalist and columnist for the Birmingham News, The Huntsville Times, and the Press-Register

John Archibald is a Pulitzer- winning columnist in the American South where he has worked for more than 35 years. He writes for the Alabama Media Group, and his columns appear in The Birmingham News, The Huntsville Times, the Mobile Press-Register, AL.com and its social brand, Reckon. John is also a national Murrow Award-winning podcaster, a voice of the deep South and what that place means to America. He is the author of the critically acclaimed memoir, Shaking the Gates of Hell: A Search for Family and Truth in the Wake of the Civil Rights Revolution, published by Alfred A. Knopf in 2021 and included as one of NPR's favorite books of the year. More recently, John was a Nieman Fellow at Harvard University in 2020-2021, and taught column writing at Harvard Summer School. While at Harvard he studied alternative storytelling and how algorithms in digital news affect perceptions of crime and contribute to polarization. Archibald's reporting has been honored more than 75 times in state and national journalism contests, including those sponsored by NABJ, the National Education Press Association, The AP, Alabama Press Association, Troy State University and others. He was honored for "distinguished journalism" by Auburn University, and enshrined on the student journalism hall of fame by the University of Alabama, his alma mater. He worked on teams that twice were finalists for IRE Awards, and his reporting led to changes in laws and policies, and the arrests and convictions of several public officials and their associates. He has appeared frequently on national and international news programs, and as a speaker at schools, colleges, conferences and clubs.

2:00 p.m. BOARD TRANSPORTATION FOR BCRI TOUR
Birmingham Civil Rights Institute - Transportation will be provided and announced at the conference.

The Birmingham Civil Rights Institute, part of the Birmingham Civil Rights National Monument and an affiliate of the Smithsonian

Institution, is a cultural and educational research center that promotes a comprehensive understanding of the significance of civil rights developments in Birmingham. Celebrating its 25th anniversary, BCRI reaches more than 150,000 individuals each year through award-winning programs and services. In 2017, the BCRI was designated as part of a Birmingham Civil Rights National Monument, along with the A.G. Gaston Motel, Kelly Ingram Park, the 16th Street Baptist and Bethel Baptist Churches.
The Civil Rights Institute tour will begin at 3:00 p.m. The tour will conclude at 5:00 p.m.

6:00 p.m. – NSNC Dinner in Magnolia 2, 3 and 4
The NSNC Legacy Award to Bonnie Jean Feldkamp
The NSNC Annual Contest Awards Announcements

Hospitality Suite will open after dinner - Cypress Room, 8th Floor

Saturday, June 11, 2022

Complimentary breakfast for hotel guests in lobby restaurant: M-F: 6-9 a.m., S-S: 6:30-10 a.m.
Coffee station and light refreshments at conference room, Magnolia 2, 3, and 4 at 8:00 a.m.

8:45 a.m. – Welcome
NSNC Interim Executive Director Adam Earnheardt

9:00 - 9:45 a.m. – Killing the Spider: What I learned putting down hot takes to tackle Alabama's systemic, historic problems by Kyle Whitmire

Kyle Whitmire will use the State of Denial initiative as a case study in how to do Big Picture Work. Ask yourself, what is the one thing you wouldn't mind writing about until you're dead? What are some ways to jump the gap between short term and long term memory so our work has lasting impact? Can you envision your community changing because of your work? What opportunities are there outside of words on a page? How can we incorporate audience development strategies into planning and execution? He's got answers.

Kyle is the state political commentator for the Alabama Media Group. He was previously a local political reporter for The Birmingham News, a columnist and new media editor for WELD for Birmingham, and political editor and author of the weekly "War on Dumb" column for the Birmingham Weekly.

9:45 - 10:30 a.m.- Parlay Your Expertise Into Online Teaching
Cole Imperi

Online education by columnists and bloggers offers enriching experiences different from traditional education. Discover a lucrative way to reach readers through education by adapting your niche to teaching online courses. NSNC member Cole Imperi founded The School of American Thanatology, offering education in Thanatology (death/grief), Thanabotany and Deathwork in 2020, and created a global reach of students in 21 countries through search engines and social media, not through paid advertising. She will compare online teaching platforms, offer the nuts and bolts of getting started, and will share her revenue figures for one course. You might find a larger audience through courses. There's not much difference between a loyal column reader and a student who is learning from you.

10:30 - 10:45 a.m. – Break

10:45 - 11:30 a.m. — Dramatic Changes in Self-Publishing
Jim Azevedo, Corporate Communications Manager, Draft2Digital

An indie revolution is happening and Jim Azevedo will reveal how Draft2Digital's 2022 acquisition of Smashwords is fueling a dramatic change in self-publishing. Learn the innovative ease and simplicity for creating print and digital publishing. Discover new tools for greater marketing, circulation and revenue for self-published authors, even if they are with other platforms.

11:30 a.m. to 1:00 p.m. – Lunch in the Daffodil Foyer

1:00 - 1:45 p.m. Home Style Opinion: Going Local to Slow Polarization
Dr. Joshua Darr,

Q&A moderated by Christopher Six

What happens when national politics disappears from the op-ed page?
In 2019, one newspaper decided to find out, and we worked with them
to measure the effects. In our book, Home Style Opinion, we detail
those findings: local issues filled the substantial void left by national
politics, and polarization slowed down. The future of local news needs
to include local opinion journalism, and we make the case for greater
support for this essential public forum in the midst of our local news
crisis.

1:45 - 2:30 p.m. – If Not Us, Then Who, Especially Now?
Roy S. Johnson

Roy S. Johnson, Director of Content Development, Alabama Media Group, Pulitzer Prize Commentary finalist

Q&A moderated by Tony Norman, NSNC President

A CONVERSATION about one journalist's life from mid-century America to the digital present, with stops along the way from the Tulsa massacre and the Trail of Tears to Stanford University, Savoy, Birmingham, Donald Drumpf, and beyond. Q&A moderated by NSNC President Tony Norman.

2:30 – 2:45 p.m. – Break

2:45 - 3:30 p.m. – Your WordPress Website Is Breaking You! 3 Ways to
Fight Back Today
Jonathan Wofford

If you're in a seemingly endless war with your WordPress site, victory is just ahead. Whether you need some basic strategies for building out a new site or you're a long-time WP user and need some serious help with updates, this is the session for you. Get answers to questions like Does your site have an SSL certificate? Did you know that you needed one? Have any clue about how much traffic your website gets or your conversion rates? Learn some tricks of the WordPress trade from a designer with two decades' experience in the industry. Attendees will be sent a survey a few weeks prior to the conference to better understand their background and needs.

3:30 p.m. Down time!

6:00 p.m. – Dinner & Ernie Pyle Lifetime Achievement Award to Mary C. Curtis
Magnolia Room 2, 3 and 4

The National Society of Newspaper Columnists presents the Ernie Pyle Lifetime Achievement Award to accomplished and deeply-respected columnist, Mary C. Curtis. She is an award-winning Roll Call columnist, journalist and educator based in Charlotte, N.C. and Washington, D.C. She has contributed to NBC News, NPR, The Washington Post, The Root, ESPN's The Undefeated and talks politics on WCCB-TV and NPR-affiliate WFAE in Charlotte. Curtis has worked at The New York Times, the Charlotte Observer, the Baltimore Sun, and the Associated Press, and was national correspondent for AOL's Politics Daily. Her coverage specialty is the intersection of politics, culture and race, and she has covered the 2008, 2012, 2016 and 2020 presidential campaigns. Curtis is a Senior Leader with The OpEd Project, at Yale University, Cornell University, and the Ford Foundation and at the Aspen New Voices Fellowship in Johannesburg, South Africa. She was a Nieman Fellow at Harvard University and a Kiplinger Fellow, in social media, at Ohio State.

Curtis was chosen to be included in The HistoryMakers, the single largest archival collection of its kind in the world designed to promote and celebrate the successes and to document movements, events and organizations that are important to the African American community and to American society; it is available digitally and permanently archived in the Library of Congress. Her honors include Clarion Awards from the Association for Women in Communications, awards from the National Headliners and the Society of Professional Journalists, three first-place awards from the National Association of Black Journalists, and the Thomas Wolfe Award for an examination of Confederate heritage groups. Curtis has contributed to several books, including an essay in "Love Her, Love Her Not: The Hillary Paradox." You can find her work at www.maryccurtis.com

The Ernie Pyle Lifetime Achievement Award is presented to honor a columnist who exemplifies outstanding achievement in the tradition of Ernie Pyle. In the 1930s, Pyle wrote a national travel column for Scripps-Howard News Service, carried in some 200 newspapers. In World War II, he became a renowned war correspondent, first in Europe, then the Pacific theater. Rather than writing about the official military perspective, Pyle reported first-hand accounts about soldiers, sailors, airmen and Marines. He was awarded a Pulitzer Prize in 1944, and the next year he was killed on a Pacific island during an attack. Past recipients include Maureen Dowd, Connie Schultz, Leonard Pitts Jr., Andy Rooney, Clarence Page, Dave Barry and Roger Ebert.

This year's ELPA selection committee consisted of Suzette Standring, Dave Astor and Mike Leonard. Standring said, "Mary C. Curtis's lifetime career encapsulates what columnists stand for and aspire to be: an eloquent truth-teller, unafraid of documenting what is, and creating clarity and hope of what can be." Astor said, "Mary C. Curtis has offered powerful and eloquent commentary on race, politics, culture, and other topics during her long and varied career. Adding to the strong appeal of Mary C.'s widely read columns are elements of humor and relevant experiences from her personal life." Leonard notes, "Mary C. Curtis is a consummate journalist, adept at hard news, opinion and perspective, and committed to advocacy for others. Her work with the OpEd Project demonstrates a commitment to empowering women and broadening our national dialogue. Her podcasts are of the highest order, thoughtful and extremely well-voiced. And if all of this gives you the impression she's all work and no play – you also might see her beautifully dressed and blissfully happy to hit Broadway for a musical or play."

Post Dinner – Hospitality Suite opens - The Cypress Room, 8th Floor

Sunday, June 12, 2022
8:00 a.m. General business meeting, Magnolia 2 and 3
Adjournment

Stay tuned for 2023!

FRIDAY AFTERNOON FIELD TRIP,
JUNE 10, 2022

NSNC ATTENDEES and their registered guests will enjoy a special after-hours tour of the BCRI.

(NOTE: Wearing masks will be required at the museum)

The Birmingham Civil Rights Institute, part of the Birmingham Civil Rights National Monument and an affiliate of the Smithsonian Institution, is a cultural and educational research center that promotes a comprehensive understanding of the significance of civil rights developments in Birmingham. Celebrating its 25th anniversary, BCRI reaches more than 150,000 individuals each year through award-winning programs and services. In 2017, the BCRI was designated as part of a Birmingham Civil Rights National Monument, along with the A.G. Gaston Motel, Kelly Ingram Park, the 16th Street Baptist and Bethel Baptist Churches (photo below).

NSNC conference attendees and their registered guests will leave the hotel at 2:00 p.m. on Friday, June 10, 2022 and arrive at the BCRI Gift Store to begin our tour. Attendees can also visit the historic sites within walking distance nearby. 5 p.m. return to the hotel.

THE NSNC 2022 LEGACY AWARD:
BONNIE JEAN FELDKAMP

FRIDAY EVENING, JUNE 10, 2022
THE NSNC 2022 LEGACY AWARD:
BONNIE JEAN FELDKAMP

WHAT WE LOVE about Bonnie Jean Feldkamp is how she throws herself — body, heart, and mind — into whatever she does, and always with an eye for the greater good, and giving opportunities to others. This is the foundation for her 2022 NSNC Legacy Award, which is given to a NSNC member who has made contributions and served in ways that will benefit our association's future.

In 2017 Bonnie became the NSNC Social Media Director where she strengthened the NSNC presence on Twitter, Instagram, our website, www.columnists.com, and other platforms. Her curation of content expanded our newsletter, *The Columnist,* to a twice-monthly publication. It was her idea that the second edition offer freelance leads for paid writing jobs.

Outreach, inclusion, and her gift for teamwork made the 2018 Cincinnati conference, which she also chaired, our most successful. She worked on webinars at free or minimal cost to benefit our members.

Bonnie collaborated with other organizations, such as the SPJ, and founded the NSNC Ambassador Program, where NSNC members interacted with journalism students.

The following elements make us proud and may give each of us hope because Bonnie's career conveys the reality that a professional vision can come true.

I first met Bonnie through the Erma Bombeck Writers Workshop, when she was a freelance writer, but not necessarily focused on journalism or becoming a professional columnist.

During her can-do tenure as NSNC Media Director, she applied advice gained from networking to her own writing even as she steered the NSNC with success. The NSNC grew in stature and Bonnie's experience grew in the field of opinion writing.

She resigned from the NSNC in 2021 to become the Opinion Editor with the Pulitzer Prize-winnng Louisville Courier-Journal. Now she is also an award winning syndicated columnist with Creators Syndicate.

Bonnie is an example of someone who contributed mightily to the NSNC, and by doing so, was led also to creating an outstanding career. Congratulations to our 2022 NSNC Legacy Award recipient! **(A sample column by Bonnie Jean Feldkamp follows.)**

BY SUZETTE MARTINEZ STANDRING, Director Emeritus

FAMILY, AND COUNTRY, DIVIDED

BY BONNIE JEAN FELDKAMP

MY BROTHER IS OLDER than me and when I was in high school, he worked second shift. I'd stay up waiting for him to get home and we'd work on jigsaw puzzles on the floor of his bedroom late into the night.

Later, we went through divorces at the same time, and we helped each other through our hard times. That was 15 years ago. We've both since remarried and I moved away. Something changed between us along the way, and I somehow missed it. I thought we were just living our lives in different towns. Our values had landed on different sides of the political aisle, but I can't say for certain that's why we don't talk anymore.

He has COVID-19 now. I went to his Facebook profile and was glad to find a public post about his symptoms and how he was doing. As I scrolled through what was public on his feed, I read a meme about blocking people on social media. It wasn't directed at me; he unfriended me years ago. But it gave me an answer to how he felt. The post read, "if you're blocked ... I don't want to see your name, hear your voice, read your words and I don't care what you're doing."

That's the hardest part. When it comes to hashing it out so we can be siblings again, I'm just not worth it to him. Cutting me out of his life and moving forward was his better option. I don't think he likes the person I grew up to become and perhaps he prefers the echo chamber that like-minded people can provide.

I fear what has happened between my brother and me is happening everywhere in our country. Hard lines are drawn, communication stops and we no longer seek common ground. We live between the layers of us and them, right and wrong. We live in a space that cannot find resolutions beyond accountability and blame. We don't want relationships, we want vindication. We've moved from an understanding that people may think differently to labeling people good or bad.

Changing hearts and minds has to come from a willingness to first listen to the other person's starting point.

Deeyah Khan made the documentary, "White Right: Meeting the Enemy." It's about the time she spent with white supremacists. She is a Muslim woman who understands the process and the necessity of really listening. Her willingness to listen did not mean she justified or excused a belief system that she vehemently disagreed with. She listened to better understand. She believes this process, though slow, can be more effective at counteracting hate. And three years after meeting a leader of a white supremacy group and featuring him in her documentary, he has left the group. Incredibly, knowing Deeyah Khan inspired his change of heart.

If we cannot figure out how to start listening, our families and communities will remain divided, and progress will only happen in response to tragedy and eruptions in our streets. What we cannot express in productive conversation we will weaponize instead.

I struggle with the fact that my brother is unvaccinated and sick with COVID-19. But I have no control over his vaccination decisions. No matter what, I treasure every good time we've had together, both as young kids and as adults. I'm grateful he was my brother when he was willing to be.

I know the odds are he'll recover, but I'm still worried I might lose him. Even if the truth is I already have.

BONNIE JEAN FELDKAMP *is the Opinion Editor with Pulitzer Prize-winning Louisville Courier-Journal and an award-winning syndicated columnist with Creators Syndicate. Find Bonnie on social media @WriterBonnie or at WriterBonnie.com.*

MARY C. CURTIS JOINS THE NSNC'S LIST OF LIFETIME LUMINARIES

BY DAVE ASTOR, NSNC ARCHIVIST

SATURDAY EVENING, JUNE 11, 2022

THE WINNER of the National Society of Newspaper Columnists' 2022 Ernie Pyle Lifetime Achievement Award is...Mary C. Curtis.

Mary C. – who is receiving the honor during this NSNC conference in Birmingham, Alabama – has had a long and varied career that's still going strong as she continues to offer powerful and eloquent commentary on race, politics, culture, and other matters during this contentious, news-heavy time. Her widely read Roll Call column also appealingly mixes in humor and personal elements.

That column is only one aspect of Mary C.'s extensive résumé. She hosts the Roll Call podcast "Equal Time with Mary C. Curtis," has been a commentator on many TV shows, and is a Senior Leader with The OpEd Project, among many other things.

"Thank you so much for this incredible honor and for placing me in such an illustrious group of winners," said Mary C. "Receiving it from peers I respect is icing on the cake."

NSNC President Tony Norman added, "If it's possible to be a super fan of a fellow columnist, then I'm Mary C. Curtis' No. 1 groupie. As much as I admire – and envy – her considerable accomplishments as a journalist and commentator, I absolutely adore her on a personal level.

"I usually only get to see her at our annual conferences," continued the Pittsburgh Post-Gazette columnist, "but when we do reconnect, it's always a thrill because she always comes bearing journalistic wisdom or interesting stories at the very least.

"I'm beyond thrilled that Mary C. Curtis, our elegant and stalwart colleague, has been named the 2022 Ernie Pyle Lifetime Achievement winner."

Mary C. – who covered the 2020, 2016, 2012, and 2008 presidential campaigns – has worked at The New York Times, Charlotte Observer, Baltimore Sun, Associated Press, and other media outlets. She has also taught at various universities, and was a Nieman Fellow at Harvard.

The winner of numerous awards has spoken three times at NSNC conferences: a solo talk in Buffalo in 2019, and as a panelist during the 2014 meeting in Washington, DC, and the 2011 gathering in Detroit.

Mary C.'s honors include Clarion Awards from the Association for Women in Communications, awards from the National Headliners and the Society of Professional Journalists, three first-place awards from the National Association of Black Journalists, and the Thomas Wolfe Award for an examination of Confederate heritage groups.

She has contributed to several books, including an essay in this year's "Covering Politics in the Age of Trump" (LSU Press), a collection from 24 top journalists. And she has been chosen for The HistoryMakers, the single largest collection – archived in the Library of Congress – that promotes successes and documents events important to the African-American community and American society.

Past winners of the 1993-founded Pyle honor – named after the renowned columnist who died while covering World War II – include

Dave Barry, David Broder, Art Buchwald, Maureen Dowd, Roger Ebert, Ellen Goodman, Pete Hamill, Molly Ivins, Steve Lopez, Mary McGrory, Clarence Page, Kathleen Parker, Leonard Pitts Jr., William Raspberry, Andy Rooney, Connie Schultz, and George Will, among others.

A 2019 NSNC interview with Mary C. can be seen on our Columnists.com site.

(A SAMPLE COLUMN **by Mary C. Curtis follows.**)

ROLL CALL

BY MARY C. CURTIS

12/09/2021
https://rollcall.com/2021/12/09/careless-adults-take-note-children-will-listen-children-will-see/

Careless adults take note: 'Children will listen … children will see'
Where Sondheim got it right and America gets it all wrong

"Careful the things you say
Children will listen
Careful the things you do
Children will see
And learn."

AT HIS DEATH late last month at the age of 91, composer and lyricist Stephen Sondheim was praised for writing for character rather than the hit parade. Playwright Arthur Laurents, who worked with him on several productions, once said Sondheim "writes a lyric that could only be sung by the character for which it was designed."

However, the audience for his work is everyone.

At this moment, the words of "Children Will Listen" from "Into the

Woods" sadly resonate in a country where children are learning the wrong lessons from adults who should know better.

In Michigan, family, friends and classmates are mourning Madisyn Baldwin, Tate Myre, Hana St. Juliana and Justin Shilling, killed in an attack in a place that should be safe, high school. A 15-year-old is charged in the murders at Oxford High School, and in a rarity, his parents are charged with involuntary manslaughter for what prosecutors say is behavior that makes them complicit.

"Guide them along the way
Children will glisten
Children will look to you
For which way to turn..."

According to Oakland County Prosecutor Karen McDonald and state authorities, the parents bought a gun that their son called "my new beauty," Mom spent time testing it out with him and, in a text told him, "LOL I'm not mad at you ... you have to learn not to get caught," when teachers found him searching online for ammunition. Perhaps realizing too late the seriousness of the tragedy her son is charged with unleashing, she allegedly texted him, "Don't Do It."

When the shooting started, Dad called authorities to tell them it could be his missing gun -- and his son.

Both parents met with school officials the morning pf the shooting and advised his behavior warranted immediate counseling, but apparently resisted taking him home or to get him the "help" the accused asked for in a disturbing note.

The teen-aged Kyle Rittenhouse was judged not guilty in Wisconsin, and walked free after killing two men and seriously wounding a third. His mother, Wendy, was never charged and has said she didn't really know what he was doing the night he traveled to Kenosha to patrol the streets holding a weapon. But where was the judgment of a parent who accompanied her teen son to a bar where he and Proud Boys drank and celebrated? Come to think of it, where were the voices chanting "what about the culture" and "where is the father," questions always posed when a youth of color does far less than shoot and kill two people?

For years because of pressure from the NRA, gun rights groups and lawmakers, Federal money for gun research from the Centers for

Disease Control and Prevention to "advocate or promote gun control" pretty much dried up. Now, some research has been re-instated, just as studies from Everytown for Gun Safety, which advocates for gun control, has found that the COVID-19 pandemic has intensified the impact of the U.S. gun violence crisis.

Very few Americans are denying anyone's right to own a gun -- for protection, for hunting, for target practice. But is common sense too much to expect?

Where indeed was the sense or the empathy when, just days after the Oxford High shooting, Rep. Thomas Massie, R-Kentucky, posted a holiday photo on Twitter, with family members of all ages smiling while displaying guns. The caption: "Merry Christmas! ps. Santa, please bring ammo."

Massie's Tweet got some support but also critics, such as Fred Guttenberg, whose 14-year-old daughter Jaime was killed in the 2018 Parkland high school shooting in Florida and who has become a gun control activist. In response to Massie's message, Guttenberg Tweeted the a photo he took of his smiling child and an image of her gravesite.

One lawmaker moved to outrage by the Michigan school shooting was Sen. Chris Murphy, D-Connecticut, whose speech just after he learned the news was certainly informed by his passion for stricter gun control laws and the Sandy Hook elementary school shooting in his own state that killed 26 people, including 20 little children, in 2012. "It happens here, in America," he said, "because we choose to let it happen."

Will more parents and lawmakers be as outraged over school shootings that are becoming shockingly routine as they seem to be about teaching children anything about America's sometimes violent history and how it could teach its citizens to do and be better?

Acknowledging facts, it is charged, could ruin a child's innocence.

These are children for whom active shooter drills have become as much a part of the curriculum as English, math and chemistry.

At Oxford high in Michigan, as a classroom of terrified students hid, there was a knock on the door, and from the other side came a voice who indicated he was friend, not foe. The suspicious students did not believe him and decided to instead take their chances by escaping out a window.

It turns out it really was law enforcement on the side of the door.

But who could blame high-schoolers for their lack of trust in people who are supposed to know best, who have promised and failed to protect them?

These children -- and to me they are children – lost their innocence a long time ago, if they ever had it.

"Careful the spell you cast
Not just on children.
Sometimes the spell may last
Past what you can see
And turn against you."

MARY C. *Curtis has worked at The New York Times, The Baltimore Sun, The Charlotte Observer, as national correspondent for Politics Daily, and is a senior facilitator with The OpEd Project. Follow her on Twitter @mcurtisnc3.*

CQ ROLL CALL'S *newest podcast,* "Equal Time with Mary C Curtis," *examines policy and politics through the lens of social justice. Please* subscribe on Apple, Spotify *or wherever you get your podcasts.*

National Society of **Newspaper Columnists**
Organization for writers of serial essay, including columnists & bloggers, in any medium

2022 CONFERENCE SPEAKERS NSNC CONFERENCE

Thursday–Saturday, June 9–12, 2022 Birmingham, AL

JOHN ARCHIBALD IS a Pulitzer- winning columnist in the American South where he has worked for more than 35 years. He writes for the Alabama Media Group, and his columns appear in *The Birmingham News*, *The Huntsville Times*, the *Mobile Press-Register*, AL.com and its social brand, Reckon. John is also a national Murrow Award-winning podcaster, a voice of the deep South and what that place means to America. He is the author of the critically acclaimed memoir, *Shaking the Gates of Hell: A Search for Family and Truth in the Wake of the Civil Rights Revolution*, published by Alfred A. Knopf in 2021 and included as one of NPR's favorite books of the year. More recently, John was a Nieman Fellow at Harvard University in 2020-2021, and taught column writing at Harvard Summer School. While at Harvard he studied alternative storytelling and how algorithms in digital news affect perceptions of crime and contribute to polarization. Archibald's reporting has been honored more than 75 times in state and national journalism contests, including those sponsored by NABJ, the National Education Press Association, The AP, Alabama Press Association, Troy State University and others. He was honored for "distinguished journalism" by Auburn University, and enshrined on the student journalism hall of fame by the University of Alabama, his alma mater. He worked on teams that twice were finalists for IRE Awards, and his reporting led to changes in laws and policies, and the arrests and convictions of several public officials and their associates. He has appeared frequently on national and international news programs, and as a speaker at schools, colleges, conferences and clubs.

JIM AZEVEDO IS the Corporate Communications Manager at Draft2Digital, having joined the company in March 2022 as part of the Smashwords acquisition. As marketing director at Smashwords since

2011, Jim helped the company grow from representing 35,000 indie authors and publishers who released 80,000 titles, to more than 150,000 authors and publishers who published over 590,000 titles. Draft2Digital offers a broad suite of free and powerful automated and self-serve tools that authors and publishers can use to build and grow their publishing businesses. This includes tools to simplify ebook and print publishing, distribution, metadata management, and marketing. Following its acquisition of Smashwords, Draft2Digital now serves more than 250,000 authors and publishers who collectively publish over 800,000 books worldwide. Visit Draft2Digital at www.draft2digital.com or follow on Twitter @Draft2Digital.

MEREDITH CUMMINGS, MJE, is an award-winning freelance multimedia journalist who coordinates #press4education for the Society of Professional Journalists, and is a member of SPJ's Journalism Education Committee. She directs the National Elementary Schools Press Association, the Alabama Scholastic Press Association and the Multicultural Journalism Workshop at The University of Alabama, where she is a full-time Senior Instructor. She is an editing consultant for WVUA 23, a professional commercial TV station. An avid college football fan, Cummings co-hosts the football show Sky Box on WVUA 90.7 each fall and produced Hissy Fit, an intergenerational podcast with her daughter Isabel. She writes columns that have appeared in various outlets, as well as in her Medium publication Woman of a Certain Rage. Reach her @merecummings on all social media.

DR. JOSHUA DARR is an assistant professor of political communication in the Manship School of Mass Communication and the Department of Political Science at Louisiana State University. He researches the influence of media on political attitudes and behavior, with a particular focus on local media, partisan polarization, and political campaigns. He received his Ph.D. in political science from the University of Pennsylvania in 2015.

LORI B. DUFF is a practicing attorney since 1994 and an award-winning author of four humor collections, including her latest, If You Did What I Asked in the First Place, which won the Foreword Indies Gold Medal. She is the vice president of the National Society of Newspaper Columnists and writes a bi-weekly column called "Legalese," which explains legal concepts by translating them into plain English. In 2020, she won first place in humor writing in the NSNC's annual column contest. Lori describes herself as an unrepentant proponent of the Oxford comma and the two-spaces-after-a-period rule. She is a part-time municipal judge and the current president of the Georgia Council of Municipal Court Judges. She lives near Atlanta and has two adult children, three if you count her husband.

BONNIE JEAN FELDKAMP is a wife and mother of three kids, whose ages span two decades. She adores Erma Bombeck, and the Clooney she most admires is George's dad, Nick — the journalist of the family, from her hometown of Cincinnati, Ohio. Bonnie Jean's award-winning columns often seek to understand how current events and family life intersect. She ties personal experiences to social issues to help readers empathize, relate and care. Bonnie Jean is the Opinion Editor for the Pulitzer Prize-winning Louisville Courier-Journal. She is also an ambassador for the National Society of Newspaper Columnists. As a writer, wife and mother, the importance of strong community resources speaks to her both personally and professionally. Journalism is a vital community resource to which she is honored to contribute. Find Bonnie Jean on social media @WriterBonnie, or learn more about her at Writer-Bonnie.com.

COLE IMPERI IS A TRIPLE-CERTIFIED THANATOLOGIST, a two-time TEDx speaker, and one of America's leading experts on death, dying, and grief. She is founder of the School of American Thanatology, which has students from 21 countries across 12 time zones. She served as the President of the 176-year-old Historic Linden Grove Cemetery & Arboretum in Covington, Kentucky, works with death-related businesses through her consulting firm, Doth, and publishes death and loss-related content as the American Thanatologist. Her new book, *A Guide to Your Grief*, will be published through Kids Can Press in 2023. She is a member of the NSNC.

ROY S. JOHNSON is Pulitzer Prize commentary finalist with the Alabama Media Group. He's the son of a Tulsa massacre survivor and is part Chocktow Indian. Roy was also able to trace his lineage to a slave in the 1700s. He grew up in Tulsa, but left for Stanford University in the 1970s and made his way to various newspapers and magazines throughout the country in the 1980s-2000s. He was the founding editor of *Savoy* magazine, a publication about "sophisticated Black life." He was primarily a sports journalist and columnist. In 2014, he landed in Birmingham and took on general columnist duties and hasn't looked back.

TONY NORMAN IS AN AWARD-WINNING COLUMNIST, associate editor, and book review editor at the Pittsburgh Post-Gazette, and is the current president of the NSNC. He began his career at the PG in 1988 as a clerk before rising to the pop music/pop culture beat a year later. In 1996, Tony became a general-interest columnist who specializes in writing about race, culture, and politics. In 1999, he was appointed to the PG's editorial board. In 2002, Tony became an adjunct professor of journalism at Chatham University where he continues to teach. In 2005, he won a Knight-Wallace Fellowship and spent a year at the University of Michigan. In 2012, Tony took on added duties as the PG's book review page editor.

REBECCA REGNIER IS AN AWARD-WINNING JOURNALIST, television host, humor columnist, author, and video content creator. She is the author of cozy mysteries as Rebecca Regnier and suspense thrillers as Rebecca Rane. Her novels in both genres have topped several Amazon charts. Her humor videos have gone viral, racking up millions of views on TikTok and Facebook. She writes a monthly humor column for The Extra Mile. Her work has been honored by the Associated Press, the National Academy of Television Arts & Sciences, the National Society of Newspaper Columnists, and the Association of Women in Communications. She lives in Michigan with her husband, sons, and incredibly handsome dog. Visit her at rebeccaregnier.com

CHRISTOPHER SIX IS a passionate advocate of community journalism with more than 30 years in the media, corporate communications and marketing. An award-winning designer, columnist, illustrator, photographer and newsroom leader, Chris is a respected voice in journalism ethics. A veteran reporter, he has created and taught news writing seminars for community colleges and the Pennsylvania Newspaper Association.

KYLE WHITMIRE IS the state political commentator for the Alabama Media Group. He was previously a local political reporter for *The Birmingham News*, a columnist and new media editor for *WELD for Birmingham*, and political editor and author of the weekly "War on Dumb" column for the *Birmingham Weekly*.

JONATHAN WOFFORD IS A MASTER PROBLEM-SOLVER, who loves tinkering away at issues he hasn't yet faced. And, most importantly, he isn't afraid to think them over and over until the correct answer is on the table. This is why he founded Your WP Guy — a WordPress tech support company – so that he can use his passion for problem-solving to help website owners have peace of mind knowing their website is safe and secure.

Ernie Pyle

LEGACY FOUNDATION

ERNIE PYLE LEGACY FOUNDATION

Erma Bombeck Writers' Workshop

The Association of LGBT Journalists

Carol Dawson
    Lori Duff
    Adam Earnheardt
    Karen Feld
    Dr. Daniela Gitlin
    Rose Goldberg
    Mary Lucille Hayes
    John Heimburg
    Chuck Keller
    Mike Leonard
    Dave Lieber
    Ginny McCabe
    Tony Norman
    Christopher Six
    Suzette Martinez Standring
    Bill Tammeus
    Beverly Ward

WE WELCOME attendees Sira Ambrosecchia and Bill Broich, whose columns do not appear.

NOTE:
    Column by Mary C. Curtis follows her EPLA announcement
    Column by Bonnie Jean Feldkamp follows her Legacy Award announcement

THE EXTRA MILER – SOUTHERN INDIANA SHOWING RESPECT FOR TOM STALEY

BY CAROL DAWSON, PRESIDENT, EEO GUIDANCE, INC.

www.eeoguidance.com
Owner, Broken Hearts, Inc.
Jonisheart.com | Freelance Writer |
Phone: 812-284-2993 | email: cdawson@eeoguidance.com

OCCASIONALLY YOU MEET a person whose kind and caring heart is immediately evident. Tom Staley was that person for all who knew him. He was my son's father-in-law and the kind of individual that we should all aspire to be.

Tom had cancer. He fought it bravely and without complaint until his body let him down. His wife, Janet, his three daughters, their families, and many friends, buried Tom on March 21, 2022.

During the funeral, a close friend commented that in the lifetime he had been friends with Tom, he had never heard a negative word said about him, but more importantly, he never heard Tom say anything bad about others. Tom Staley was clearly loved, respected, and admired.

After the heart-warming and sorrowful goodbyes at Tom's crowded funeral, it was time to make the long trip to the gravesite for final words and a special Veteran tribute by the Sellersburg American Legion Post 204.

My husband and I, along with our young grandsons, were one of the last cars in the long procession to Tom's final resting place. We quickly noticed every vehicle pulled to the side of the road (on both sides), and stopped at traffic lights; some vehicles waiting through multiple light changes as the procession headed from Sellersburg to New Albany. Throughout the 10-minute drive, it was inspiring and emotional to see how Southern Indiana citizens showed their respect and reverence toward the funeral procession.

Members of the American Legion were at the gravesite to greet the Navy Veteran and those who loved him. The ceremony consisted of the playing of "Taps," a rifle detail with a gun salute, a touching poetry reading, and uniformed service members presentation of the burial flag. It was a sobering ceremony as the flag was methodically and reverently folded and placed into the hands of Tom's grieving widow.

Tom Staley, the Navy Veteran who always went the extra mile in both his personal and professional life, courageously fought his final battle with cancer. Although we grieve his loss, it is now time for our friend to rest in peace. His pain is gone.

Matthew 5:4 "Blessed are those who mourn, for they will be comforted."

KINDNESS TIPS: If you are in a vehicle and see a funeral procession (typically the cars will follow a black sedan/hearse and have a flag and/or emergency flashing lights), slow your vehicle, pull to the side of the road, and wait until all cars in the procession pass. If you are a pedestrian, stop walking and remove your hat if you're wearing one.

THE AMERICAN LEGION **posts throughout the US are in need Veterans willing to help in various capacities with funerals. If you are a military Veteran, please consider talking with the American Legion in your area to find how you might help with future Veteran funeral proceedings. Don't let this ceremony honoring our Veterans vanish because of lack of volunteers.**

· · ·

CAROL A. DAWSON is a resident of Jeffersonville and owner of EEO GUIDANCE, Inc. If you have seen or been a part of an act of kindness or know an EXTRA MILER, please let her know about it. To submit a story or act of kindness, contact Carol via email: Cdawson@eeoguidance.com or mail: THE EXTRA MILERS, 212 Pearl Street, Jeffersonville, IN 47130.

FROZEN DINNERS

BY LORI DUFF

Published February 22, 2022
(https://www.loriduffwrites.com)

BACK IN THE day before microwaves and an entire aisle in the grocery store wasn't dedicated to frozen meals of increasing gourmet pretensions, there was the TV Dinner. TV dinners were packaged and served on a divided foil plate. You had your meat, smothered in some kind of gravy or sauce, and decidedly not shaped like it came directly from the animal. Then there was a vegetable, usually wrinkly green peas, some kind of starch like a perfectly square corn muffin or a half-dozen French fries, and a dessert. The dessert was either chocolate pudding or some variation on apple pie. The dessert always had a stray pea hiding in it.

They felt like astronaut meals. The foil tray was shiny like a space-suit. TV Dinners were real food, in that you could eat them and they tasted more or less like their non-TV dinner counterparts, but they were also not real. The meat was mashed and reconstituted. The potatoes were a little too uniform. The vegetables seemed freeze-dried in addition to frozen. If you ate the dessert first, you'd blister your tongue. Despite being pre-made, they weren't instant gratification food. They had to be cooked from frozen in a preheated oven.

These days, I usually eat leftovers for lunch. I am incapable of cooking for one, or two, or even four. I have my mother's habit of cooking enough for each meal to feed an army of angels who may decide to descend upon my doorstep and need sustenance. I suppose I could learn to halve the ingredients, but I prefer my own cooking to freezer food. I like leftovers. Every once in a while, though, I end up with a commercial frozen meal. The other day I ate something that promised to contain organic, flash frozen vegetables. I showed it to my friend, Diane, and pointed out how far frozen food had come since those TV Dinners.

Thinking of that, I wondered if the originals were still available. The next time I found myself in a grocery store, I bought one. The selection was slim, overwhelmed by restaurants offering up a frozen version of their popular entrees and a variety of meals that promised great health and weight loss. I finally found the Hungry Man dinners, which were shaped like the originals, but with the tray plastic instead of foil for the microwave.

I wanted Salisbury Steak, since that seemed the TV-iest of all dinners, but they didn't have any. Instead, I got chicken-fried chicken, which had two perfectly oval fried chicken patties covered in an Elmer's glue-like gravy. It had mashed potatoes, green beans, and a tiny portion of stewed apples cut into perfect squares. I am pleased to say that the apples did not have any vegetables in them whatsoever.

I only glanced at the nutrition value, long enough to see that I didn't want to know any more. You'd think with all that salt (75% of my daily dose of sodium) the meal would have more flavor, but you'd be wrong. I can't say it was good, but if I'm going to be honest I have to say I liked it a fair bit better than asparagus, nature's nastiest vegetable.

I ate it anyway. I was hungry, man, and it was lunchtime.

Mostly, I think I enjoyed the nostalgia. The last time I ate an honest-to-God TV dinner Jimmy Carter was president and I had no responsibilities in the world beyond cleaning my room when my parents demanded it. Going outside to ride my bike nowhere in particular, or just around and around the cul-de-sac was a valid activity. I had to stop playing to eat my Salisbury Steak and mashed potatoes with a little peak on top, as if they'd been served out of a soft-serve ice cream machine. Our 19-inch TV, the one we ate them in front of, was the fancy big one.

Maybe, instead of reaching back to those times with a TV Dinner, I should just go outside and play. I wonder if I can still ride a bike with no hands or roller skate without killing myself. If it turns out that I can't do either of those things, maybe they'll serve Salisbury Steak at the hospital. It is easy to chew, after all.

LORI B. DUFF
    https://www.loriduffwrites.com
    Ghost writer, writing consultant, general fun person to be around
    National Society of Newspaper Columnists Vice President
    2019 Foreword INDIE Awards Gold Medal Winner
    NSNC Column Contest 2020 First Place Winner and 2018 &
2019 Honorable Mention Recipient
    2020 Georgia Author of the Year Nominee
    New Apple 2017 Official Selection
    Readers' Favorite 2017 Bronze Medal Winner

(NOTE: I would be remiss if I didn't mention Elaine Ambrose's memoir, Frozen Dinners: A Memoir of a Fractured Family: Elaine Ambrose: 9781612542843: Amazon.com: Books

WHY I (PROBABLY REALLY) STARTED PLAYING FORTNITE AT 51

BY ADAM EARNHEARDT FOR MAHONING MATTERS

THE EARNHEARDTS
Published February 21, 2022

MOST MEN in their 50s are not gamers. At least not the guys I know. We 50-somethings don't even look like gamers. We're not even close to the image one conjures when asked to picture a gamer.

INSTEAD, MENTION "GAMER" and an image of a prepubescent with eyeballs fixed on a screen, holding a controller or a mouse in one hand while the other clicks away at a keyboard, head adorned with earphones and mic, surrounded by empty pop cans, chip bags, chocolate bar and candy wrappers.

It looks bad. It looks slothful. Of course, we now know it's anything but lazy. For gamers, it's a real sport, maybe even an art form. In most cases, it's positively a social environment for kids. They're in it for fun. Some are playing for glory, clout and even cash.

But that's not me. I suck at these games. I don't win much. When I do, it's a sad display of contorted dance moves meant to serve as gloating the likes my wife hasn't seen since I played beer league softball. What's even sadder is that the only ones there to see it are my wife and 9-year-old son. They laughed at first. Now they just look at me with pity.

So then, "How did I end up here?" you might ask. At 51, why have I been playing Fortnite every day for the last two months? Yes, I know I don't resemble the typical gamer. Most people won't think of an overweight, bald, out-of-shape, Gen X-er with a voice as deep as Leonard Cohen's going toe-to-toe with some stripling gamer halfway around the world.

Plus, whoever that little kid is, she or he usually kicks my ass.

No. I'm most definitely not in it for glory or cash.

The path to my gamerdom probably doesn't seem all that unusual. Still, my motivations don't align with that of a traditional gamer. This is because I started playing to connect with my son. And, if I'm being completely honest, I started playing because it looked like fun.

Quite frankly, it's a weird environment for someone my age. I didn't know this going into my recent gaming foray, but I'm absolutely, positively the oddball on Fortnite. Yes, there are a lot of kids in this game. A lot. It's rated T for Teens, but I get the sense there are more kids my son's age than actual "teens" playing this game. According to Dot Esports, the "T" rating simply means the game is appropriate for players 13 years old and older, and that parents of younger kids should consider this when allowing them to play the game.

This is exactly what we did as the parents of a 9-year-old obsessive Fortniter. We had (and still have) long talks with Ozzie about game play, about who is playing, and about making smart choices when interacting with others in the game.

Still, therein lies a big problem for the gamer guy in his 50s. There are options for playing the game with a headset and microphone because you can team up with other players. Playing Fortnite in squads (groups of four) is a popular option among the young gamers. You're expected to communicate with these other players. Of course, they all sound like my son and not Johnny Cash. So I can't very well drop my deep, bassy Dad voice into the open chat.

Sorry. I know creepy when I hear it. That's a strange boundary I won't cross.

When my 9-year-old son started playing, he was motivated by the connection to his friends. It was a way to hang out after school. I lurked over his shoulder, convinced that some weirdo would try to friend him. If I heard a voice like mine on the other end, I'd have questions. Lots of questions. So I can't (I won't) play Fortnite like the rest of them unless they suddenly come up with a special "over 30" league for us old-timers.

Yes, I just called you 30-somethings "old timers" (at least I didn't call you "Boom…" oh never mind).

But when Ozzie played, that didn't happen. No stranger danger, at least not yet.

I know his friends and they know Dad isn't only looking on, he's playing. Although I'm sure there are weirdo predators out there who mean to do harm to kids like my son, this looked like a safe enough environment, in part because I was part of it — even if it was a bit strange when my son's friends started to send me friend requests. I politely declined, by the way (or maybe I ignored them; I don't remember).

Looking on with concerned parent eyes while Ozzie played, I got hooked. There was an ease with which I adapted to the gameplay, which was very important for someone who doesn't have the same fine psychomotor skills of a 9 year-old. This is important because I'm an old guy who finds escape in a kids game. Some people my age have other hobbies to release and unwind after a particularly stressful or busy day. Maybe it's exercise or a good book. Maybe it's TV or music. Maybe it's a long hike through Mill Creek Park.

My stress reliever — at least, right now — just happens to be a game I downloaded to the Nintendo Switch (fun side note: it's actually my Nintendo Switch, a 50th birthday present from my kids because I was always stealing their Switch to play The Legend of Zelda: Breath of the Wild. But I digress.) It's been good for me, for my mental health, for my connection to my son.

In fact, playing Fortnite has had two very positive outcomes.

First, my son feels more connected to me. My daughters are Fortnite haters. They hate everything associated with the game and think it's quite hilarious that Dad is now a Fortniter. Now Ozzie has someone at home who cares about Fortnite almost as much as he does. He is wrapped up in the lore of Fortnite, the stories that surround the game. Before my interest, he only had his friends to share those stories with. Now he has me, and I love to hear that little voice share his views of the world with me (even the virtual ones).

Apparently, I'm late to the party because there are many stories of past chapters and seasons I've missed. He feels like he's teaching me important facts, even though I know those stories won't really help me play the game.

He's pretty darn good at it, both playing the game and in the telling of Fortnite lore. He wants me to learn all the characters and their histories and repeat them back to him. He quizzes me from time to time, and I'm proud to say, I'm starting to pick it up (even if it does nothing to help me earn a victory crown in a solo match).

This storytelling is the best part of how he and I share in the experience. We went to a YSU basketball game and he spent the entire first half telling me about Fortnite, clearly uninterested in the awesome game that was being played right in front of him. But he had my undivided attention, and that was more important than a few slam dunks and a YSU win.

The second outcome is a little harder to describe but equally important to my mental health.

I get excited when I win in Fortnite. My blood pumps a little faster when I take a victory crown or level up after finishing an important quest. As inconsequential as it sounds (and trust me, I know how it sounds), I feel like I've accomplished something.

People my age tend to become more nostalgic as we get older, looking back on lives fulfilled personally and professionally, reviewing timelines for triumphant moments, scanning for pictures of our past that make us reminisce, smile and cry. We do this because we want to rekindle feelings of youth, maybe grasping at faded memories of sitting in front of a large TV screen playing Mike Tyson's Punch-Out!! on the original Nintendo or maybe Pac-Man on an Atari 2600 console or Pong.

It doesn't matter what the games are, because what really matters is that playing them makes me feel like a kid again. When I play, I feel a little immature, in a good way, if even for a few minutes. When I play games and the virtual world gets a little intense, I like the feelings of euphoric stress, like watching the ending of a close sports game or the climax of a scary movie — a good kind of stress that excites the senses.

Sure. I started playing Fortnite because it was a fun, exciting way to reconnect to my childhood. Maybe even to unwind a little. But the fact that I can play as a way to connect with my kid is hands-down the only victory crown, clout or quest reward I'll ever need.

ADAM EARNHEARDT IS *professor of communication at YSU, executive director of the Youngstown Press Club, and interim executive director of the National Society of Newspaper Columnists. Follow him on Twitter at @adamearn.*

FIRST MARCHING ORDERS
MARINE BAND

BY KAREN FELD

PoliticalMavens.com
Published 1/21/2021
www.karenfeld.com | mobile: 202 236-0047

THE UNITED STATES Marine Band is truly what Thomas Jefferson called it, "The President's Own."

President George W. Bush took that literally when he once surprised the 2,600 guests at the annual White House Correspondents' Association dinner by conducting the Marine Band in a medley of patriotic compositions, and although sometimes missing the beat, receiving a standing ovation for his leadership ability in that area.

The band has played at almost every presidential Inauguration and State Dinner since its White House debut on New Year's Day, 1801. It played when Lincoln delivered the Gettysburg Address, at Grover Cleveland's White House wedding and at President John F. Kennedy's funeral. Ronald Reagan once called the Marine Band "a national institution and a national treasure."

The primary purpose of America's oldest professional music group is to provide music and pageantry for the president and the commandant of the Marine Corps. "Given our mission, we work for whoever is in the office," says clarinetist and Colonel Jason Fettig, Director of the band. But this being a democratic country, the rest of us get to share the privilege. "The band performs in many different capacities," says Fettig, "and is enjoyed by many different audiences."

The band gives some 500 public and official performances each year — the concert on the U.S. Capitol grounds, a tradition started by President Martin Van Buren more than 160 years ago, is perhaps the best-known.

"The President's Own" plays at the White House for more than 300 occasions each year – though it may assume different forms. A half-dozen ensembles – ranging from a solo violinist in the East Room to all 143 musicians together – may play at any given State Dinner. Typically, strolling string players perform during dinner, a dance band plays after dinner and another group may play patriotic music. When the string orchestra plays, it's always in the grand foyer. Musical styles range from patriotic band selections to pieces written for smaller chamber groups.

"It's most exciting when we go to the White House to lend entertainment or atmosphere for guests," says Fettig. "It's also awe-inspiring to be on the balcony playing a concert for guests on the South Lawn."

Fettig says musicians must be able to adapt to almost any musical situation or style. Some functions call for a solo from the band's harpist, for instance; others, a full concert. "We're one large band, and from that, we can supply a chamber orchestra, a jazz band, a dance band for a state dinner, various chamber ensembles and a country music ensemble," he says. "It is a challenge to find such versatility."

As in the past, most of today's band members attended prestigious music schools. The first woman enlisted in the Marine Band in 1973. Band members are selected at highly competitive auditions, then enlist in the Marine Corps for duty solely with the Marine Band. They've got some famous shoes to fill, after all. During his dozen years with the band, beginning in 1880, bandmaster and composer John Phillip Sousa brought "The President's Own" to its standard of excellence; in 1891 he initiated the band's annual concert tour throughout the country. The band still marches frequently in the footsteps of its famous former director.

And although President Bush made a splash with his conducting debut, he wasn't offered a post-White House position leading America's oldest professional musical group who for many years have offered free weekly concerts at the marine barracks in SE DC.

Breaking tradition for President Joe Biden's Inauguration, the band members wore black masks between songs and were distanced over a larger, 90-foot platform and separated from one other by clear protective shields. But in keeping with tradition and the uplifting energy, John Philip Sousa's marches were a prominent part of the Inaugural program. The band played "Hail to the Chief," the traditional salute to the president, then proudly accompanied Lady Gaga with a rendition of "The Star Spangled Banner." And the show goes on.

SHOES: A MARRIAGE MORALITY TALE

BY DR. DANIELA GITLIN

11/4/2021
https://www.danielagitlin.com

SHOES. They're functional, sometimes fashionable, and all too often underfoot. Especially in the garage. It's house policy to leave our shoes there. Otherwise, we track dirt in, which Hubby wouldn't notice. He's also oblivious to dropped food and pens; to burnt-out light bulbs and the overflowing kitchen garbage can.

After decades of training, he now kicks off his shoes before entering the house. Usually at the base of the step-up to the door, where they're a hazard when stepping down until I toss them to the left onto his three-foot mound of cowboy boots, sandals, loafers, and running shoes. My shoes are lined up on the right—one pair of wellies, one pair of snow boots, one pair of all-weather mocs, my house slippers and the pair I wear to work.

Storage. That's my problem with Hubby's shoes. They pile up. They drift. They wander into places where they shouldn't be. How many times have I tripped over one? I adore Hubby but I'm a neatnik, he's not, and as the poet Henry Wadsworth Longfellow said: Into every life some rain must fall. Some days must be dark and dreary, you can't have it all.

What was I thinking that day I stepped down from the house into the garage without turning on the light? My ankle twisted and foot slipped off an uneven lump of shoe. I pitched forward like an axed tree, in slo-mo, klaxons wailing, newscaster narrating, "*She's go o o o ing dow ow ow ow n n n n....*" and landed, palms flat on the concrete, elbows pumping mini pushups—*boing boing boing*—till I went to ground, cheek on dirty concrete, time zipping back to normal.

Wow! What a save! I could have smashed my face. I lay there and caught my breath. Gingerly, I lifted up onto my elbows, rotated my wrists and ankles, rolled over slowly to squat, and pulled myself upright, a little dizzy. As relief faded that nothing was broken, righteous indignation welled up at Hubby, sentences writing themselves before my mind's eye—*HOW MANY TIMES do I have to ask? WHEN ARE YOU GOING TO STOP leaving your damn shoes in the line of traffic? DON'T YOU CARE*—I looked down at the guilty party. It was my shoe.

Oh, the irony! I burst out laughing. Into each life, some stupid must fall. Some days are humbling. You can't know it all.

DANIELA GITLIN IS *an NSNC member and rural psychiatrist in private practice in upstate New York. Her clinical memoir* Practice, Practice, Practice: This Psychiatrist's Life *was selected a Finalist by the 2021 International Book Awards. Her second book,* Doorknob Moments: Why

Clients Drop Shockers on Their Way Out the Door and Why You Want Them To *will be published by WW Norton in 2024. She blogs at* www.danielagitlin.com

THE YEAR OF MAGICAL ZOOMING

BY ROSE CARMEN GOLDBERG

Los Angeles Times

IT STARTED like any pandemic-era Zoom meeting. I awkwardly angled my screen toward my bedroom wall to hide the clothes littering my floor. I changed into one of my button-up Zoom shirts. I joined others on screen. A gray cat slinked across someone's keyboard. One participant struggled to turn on her video.

Then, suddenly, it felt very different.

The moderator asked everyone to say the name of their loved one who had died. "My mom, Dana." "My dad, Hal." "My friend, Laura."

Four months before that Zoom meeting, my dad had died alone in his assisted living facility in Oakland. As he declined after a stroke, I chased him from a distance. I videoed my way into rooms I could not enter because of COVID restrictions and blew him kisses from behind a glass wall. There'd been no memorial, nothing. It was as if my dad had vanished into thin air.

The hospice program that had cared for my dad encouraged me to join a virtual grief group. I declined brusquely. My loss felt so private. The last thing I wanted was to share it with strangers. Besides, Zooming about grief seemed tacky, emojis and chat boxes so incongruous with the sanctity of death.

A few weeks later, my mom called. She'd received my dad's ashes. They came in a dark box engraved with gold designs. I imagined a van full of these boxes shuttling across the country, delivering the dust of the dead like holiday packages. I pictured my mom, in her one-room apartment in Berkeley, with this box for as long as the pandemic dragged on. I was too sad to cry.

The next night, my cellphone alerted me it was running out of space. It was clogged with photos from friends in quarantine trying to text their way out of isolation. Scrolling through the photos, I came across the last one I took of my dad. He seemed real, too big for that small box. Instantly, I felt like I was holding a bomb about to detonate. I threw my phone across the room.

The next time a hospice counselor called, I said I was ready to join the virtual grief group.

I was nervous before my first meeting. I imagined I'd find Brady Bunch squares of grievers, a pixelated quilt of strange sad faces. I wondered if it made sense to sign up for more darkness. What I found, though, was heartbroken but whole people. Like me. Struggling through the pandemic and longing for a new future, while learning how to build bridges with loved ones lost to the past.

Every week a participant made a presentation about the person they had lost. We held frayed black-and-white photos of youthful smiling faces up to our screens. We shared color photos of these faces, sunken and weak. We talked about the lives lived in between.

As I showed photos of my dad, I felt suffocated by grief. Too choked up to talk, I closed my eyes. When I opened them, I saw group members crying with me. One gave me an air hug through the screen. Sitting in my bedroom alone, my loss felt shared, and lighter.

Technological glitches brought us closer, too.

One participant kept losing connectivity while trying to tell us about her mom. She frantically logged in again and again. Once she regained video, she fought futilely for sound. Her silent face caved in with pained defeat. These moments only reinforced how much we needed each other, former strangers, now friends in grief.

We shared milestones. In November, election anxiety muddied our mourning. At Thanksgiving, we hid from empty dining room chairs by eating turkey in our kitchens. Some decided not to send Christmas cards, not wanting them to be death announcements.

Our last meeting was the Monday before New Year's Eve. With a new year and a coronavirus vaccine upon us, we pondered how we would reenter the world without our loved ones. "We are in the eye of the storm, it seems like help is on the way, but what will it feel like when the world reopens and starts spinning faster?" the moderator asked us.

I felt dread. Eventually, my dad's assisted living facility will reopen to visitors. I'll be allowed to go to the common room where we used to eat cookies. But it won't matter because my dad won't be there. I'll be able to host dinners in my apartment. But my dad's chair will remain empty.

For me, my group members, and many others, I realized, the reopening of society post-quarantine will cause a second period of grief.

There was solace, though, knowing I won't be going it alone. I'll likely never see my group members again. But I'll carry them, like a blanket wrapped warm around me, a comforting reminder of the strength of human connection. Powerful enough to cross the vast virtual divide.

The final session ended unlike any other Zoom meeting I'd ever attended. The moderator angled her camera toward a table covered in candles. She lit them one by one for each person we'd lost. As we logged off, she whispered, "These candles represent your courage to comfort others. They represent the light of love."

CONTACT   **ROSE   CARMEN   GOLDBERG:** rose.carmen.goldberg@aya.yale.edu;
https://muckrack.com/rose-carmen-goldberg/portfolio/list

THE BEAUTY AND FRAGILITY OF PEACE

BY MARY LUCILLE HAYS

Letter from Birdland

THE SKY IS BLANKETED with grey, and the heavy clouds have sprinkled snow over the bare fields. The stubs of last year's cornstalks make stripes all the way back to the fence row. The sky has muted the color from the fields and woods, and the world looks like a black and white photo. I have counted at least twenty deer in the herd that marches to the west. The deer are not in a line, but they are all going the same direction across the barren field. They remind me of photos I've seen in the last days, of people fleeing the bombardments of the Russian forces in Ukraine.

This terrible news has me thinking of my dear childhood friend, Liuda. Even in childhood, Liuda was proud of her heritage. I remember feeling awed, and a little bit jealous when she and her mother would break into a Ukrainian conversation when we were out together. Liuda brought little bits of her culture to us, especially the beautifully detailed Easter eggs, painstakingly dyed in stages, like a batik. She had a group of us over to her house teaching us how to heat the kistka (a metal stylus used for drawing patterns on the eggs) in the flame of a candle. You then melt the block of beeswax with the hot kistka, pulling a bit of liquified wax into the bowl, and then draw a pattern on the egg with the wax. Not the whole pattern, of course, just the lines you want to be white at the end of the process.

Photo by Liuda Shtohryn

Ukrainian egg dyes are intense, not the pastel food coloring we used at home to create Robin's egg blue, or a rosy pink (although I love dying eggs that way, too). When you have fixed your white lines, drop the egg into the lightest color, say yellow. Then you reheat your stylus and draw all the lines and shapes you want to remain yellow. Let the wax cool and drop the egg into the next darker color. Over and over, you draw your patterns and dip your eggs in darker and darker colors until the picture is complete. When it is finished, use a candle to melt the wax from the egg, revealing your design. Picture four girls around the kitchen table, Liuda's mother supervising. The beauty of the eggs delighted us, but we discovered their fragility when one of the eggs, maybe too close to the candle's flame, exploded! Raw egg on the ceiling and on the walls! How we shrieked, and then laughed.

Unlike the eggs we dyed at home, hardboiled and eaten soon after the Easter egg hunt—deviled or in salads or even just peeled and salted, Ukrainian Easter eggs are permanent pieces of art, often passed down through the generations. Although raw eggs are used, and they can explode, more commonly they simply dry out on the inside, the gasses escaping gently. (I've seen this happen when I pocket an egg from the henhouse in the last parts of winter and forget it until I don my winter coat again the next fall. I put my hand in my pocket and pull out an egg. It is as light as an empty shell because that is what it has become.) I see images of people with suitcases and bundles and even plastic bags, trying to get to safety, and I wonder if they've had time or space to pack these delicate heirlooms.

Liuda told us that she is worried for her cousins in Ukraine and their sons. I heard that President Zelensky has asked all the men from ages 18-60 to fight. That would include all three of our sons. My husband would just barely escape the call. I can only imagine what Liuda or her cousins must be feeling. How can we help? Although we should be careful of upstart charities that may be scams, we can vet organizations to find reputable ones with some easy-to-use online tools, such as www.charitynavigator.org/. I just typed "Ukraine" into the search. They have rated these charities, and scrolling down a little, I found one with an 85% rating: "Give with confidence." Digging deeper, we can find specifics, like how much they spend on administration, fundraising, and the actual program. We can even see what percentage of their money goes to a particular mission.

The sun has risen again over clear skies and in our back field, the deer have gone. The people continue their slow progress to refuge and relative safety. The crisis continues, and I meditate on the beauty and fragility of those eggs.

CREATE BEAUTY; *Defend Peace; Blessed Be*

. . .

MARY LUCILLE HAYS

Letter from Birdland is published weekly in *The Piatt County Journal Republican* and biweekly in *The News Gazette*.

Email: letterfrombirdland@gmail.com
Instagram: @BirdlandLetters
www.letterfrombirdland.blogspot.com

THE LITTLE BOOK OF BASICS TRANSLATOR DICTIONARY

JOHN HEIMBURG, Guest Columnist, Daily Commercial - jvheimburg@comcast.net

As a public service, to try to clear up some of the confusion in our political discourse, I offer you:

The Little Book of Basics Translator Dictionary

Language Identification Codes: **Maga** = ***MAGA-Alternative language*** **SAE** = ***Standard American English***

BLACK LIVES MATTER (BLM)/ANTIFA - *1.* ***Maga*** A Marxist conspiracy to destroy America and its huge, highly armed military branch. 2. ***SAE*** People bringing awareness to the disproportionate murder with impunity of Black folks, primarily men, and a number of loosely affiliated groups who sometimes defend nonviolent protesters from vicious attacks by extremists.

Cancel Culture/Karen - *1.* ***Maga*** Innocent white folk/women who are distraught because they are facing consequences like losing their reputation or job just because they've done something despicable to dominate their social "inferiors". 2. ***SAE*** Whiny white folk/women who have no concern that Black people have been "cancelled" over the past few centuries by being lynched, burned alive or shot for the offense of demanding respect as human beings.

Critical Race Theory (CRT) - *1*. *Maga* Literally every horrible, insane thing you can think of to claim the liberals are doing to destroy our country, like fomenting hate, racism, child abuse - you name it. *2*. *SAE* A high-level law school course investigating how the legal framework of the U.S. has evolved, beginning in an epoch of legal enslavement of black humans up to the present day.

Democracy - *1*. *Maga* Mob rule. *2*. *SAE* A system of self-governance in which citizens are in charge of running their own government.

Dictatorship - *1*. *Maga* When you are required to wear a mask or get vaccinated. *2*. *SAE* When the guy in charge has absolute, unquestionable discretion over whether you live or die. Torture and imprisonment are also standard powers.

Election Security (Stolen Election) - *1*. *Maga* How to explain an over 7 million vote margin if you're a poor loser; a devious, slimy way to limit voting by black and brown folk; how to put people with high loyalty and low ethical standards in charge of counting the votes next time. *2*. *SAE* Assuring that every citizen has equitable access to voting and that their vote will be counted by people of integrity.

Freedom - *1*. *Maga* Getting things my way, even if it means using violence and intimidation. *2*. *SAE* A right we earn by not hurting other people.

Heritage - *1*. *Maga* A nostalgic remembrance of how great things used to be when white people were in overwhelming control of how everything worked. *2*. *SAE* Real memories of how things weren't so great for some people, and how they still aren't in many cases.

January 6th Insurrection - *1*. *Maga* A normal day of patriot tourists peacefully exercising legitimate political discourse. *2*. *SAE* A violent attempted coup to overturn the legitimate election of the president and re-install the loser, resulting in the sacking of the nation's capitol, injury to over 100 police officers, and the death of five people.

Law & Order - *1*. *Maga* A show of force to keep protesters "in line". *2*. *SAE* A trope used by political candidates because it sells, and it's easier than explaining or fixing the real problems.

Medical Freedom - *1*. *Maga* Not being asked about my vaccination status, even if it means infecting others. 2. **SAE** The freedom (aspirational) to receive high quality medical care that does not bankrupt me.

Patriot - *1*. ***Maga*** A person who is loyal to Dear Leader. 2. ***SAE*** One who defends and upholds our values of freedom in equality.

Q-anon - *1*. ***Maga*** A font of wisdom & truth from a great and secret patriot. 2. ***SAE*** An insane batch of conspiracies cooked up to destabilize/destroy functional democratic process.

Republic - *1*. ***Maga*** A sort of government that doesn't need to be democratic, and where a "Strong Leader" can guarantee our freedom (see **Freedom**). 2. ***SAE*** A form of government, when democratic, where the will of the people is carried out by elected representatives.

Woke - *1*. ***Maga*** Using CRT to teach our kids to hate our country and each other. 2. ***SAE*** An awareness of a political system in which some folks' lives are valued 'way more than others.

JOHN HEIMBURG, Guest Columnist, Daily Commercial - jvheimburg@comcast.net

CHUCK KELLER:

In Other Words: Exhausted By Constant Outrage Can Numb Us To Real Issues

People are cranky. We recently returned from a road trip and many of the services that we needed were short-handed. We saw lots of signs that indicated that customers took their dissatisfaction and anger out on the employee who happened to show up that day. Our world is changing quickly and those new demands put us under stress and when we are under stress, well, we do things that we will probably regret.

I'm exhausted by outrage. There it is in my newsfeed, internet posts, newspaper headlines, television shows. We should be outraged by the way humans treat each other but we should also be working to address those problems. Identifying a real issue and a manufactured issue seems to be blurring. Yelling does not fix the issue. This period of time will be known as the Age of Rage.

At first the expression of outrage seems good. We express our anger, frustration, and our moral indignity. It is often a quick reaction. But then someone will inevitably turn the topic to vengeance or harm to a perceived offender. That's when things get scary. After all, the Catholic Church was outraged with Galileo when he said that the Earth was not the center of the universe. He earned life imprisonment. It took 400 years to apologize for that one. Any more I study the person who is outraged to see, like a magician, what the other hand is doing. Outrage has become a deflection, an intentional misdirection.

Recently, my sister witnessed an event that made me think of this. We met for lunch at a little restaurant on remote Washington Island in Lake Michigan. The Internet service is spotty at best so restaurants rely on Venmo, cash, and check more than using the Internet to verify a charge. She heard the customer's frustration with the lack of service. The owner told the man to enjoy his lunch. At first the owner's comment seemed a bit callous but we later discovered that the customer was not accustomed to the island custom and wanted to pay immediately. The customer expressed his outrage at the lack of modern services but he learned that he was the target of genuine kindness. Even in overhearing part of the conversation, my sister imposed her values on an island custom and misread the situation. Once we realized the situation we were a bit embarrassed. This seems to happen in the world more often than not.

I really don't see much sense in proselytizing anger or outrage. And like anything taken to extremes, it is not constructive. It destroys things.

We can scream an outrage over any topic du jour but a situation won't get any better unless we are wiling to get in there and do something. At one point the Cuyahoga River caught fire because it was so polluted. People were outraged. But instead of just yelling about it, folks got down to work to clean up the mess. It was hard work but it happened. That outrage turned into something positive.

I'm not telling anyone what to believe or even how to behave. An essay can only examine a portion of an idea. It cannot examine a topic completely. It is thinking aloud that attempts to contribute a little to something larger. I am tired of outrage. My mother would be pleased that I now understand her admonition of "If you don't have anything nice to say, don't say it."

CONTACT   CHUCK   KELLER: cmkeller@live.com   or   visit linknky.com

JUST CALL HIM
PRESIDENT PERSPEKTIVNY

BY MIKE LEONARD

The B-Town Bee
March 2022

THE USEFUL IDIOT offered himself up as perspektivny like no one has ever seen. People say they can't believe it. So much winning. For Putin.

I'd heard Donald J. Trump called a google of names, but never "perspektivny."

"A f***ing moron," as assessed by his former Secretary of State, Rex Tillerson.

"An idiot {with the intelligence of} a kindergartener," according to former National Security Adviser, H.R. McMaster.

"Someone who 'sucks up and shits down' conservative-as-a-Fox media manager Roger Ailes allegedly said.

Actually idiot appears often in quotes attributed to people who would know. As in, this is not a paraphrase. They said idiot.

"Useful idiot" isn't a term that comes from these people. Perhaps it's the knowledge that the term acknowledges that Trump has been a Russian asset. They whisper about it but won't say it in their outdoor voices.

A useful idiot.

The attention to Trump's flailing over Putin's "genius" and the horror of Ukraine highlights the aforementioned term, perspektivny.

In-depth reporting from the The Guardian last year documented Russian President Vladimir Putin's fervent push leading up to the 2016 election to swing the United States election to Donald Trump.

"They agreed a Trump White House would help secure Moscow's strategic objectives, among them 'social turmoil' in the U.S. and a weakening of the American president's negotiating position," the British newspaper and news site reported.

An internal Russian report The Guardian obtained said Trump was the "most promising candidate". In Russian, that word is perspektivny. And it means, essentially, useful idiot.

The report also reportedly described Trump as an "impulsive, mentally unstable and unbalanced individual who suffers from an inferiority complex"

It's like they could see into his soul.

Like President Joe Biden's verbal roadmap of what Russia intended to do in Ukraine, the British publication reported Putin's objectives. "A Trump win 'will definitely lead to the destablisation (British spelling) of the US's sociopolitical system' and see hidden discontent burst into the open, it predicts'.

Putin got what he wanted. A lapdog who, incidentally, doesn't care for dogs, but barks incessantly.

Trump disowned the entire U.S. intelligence community when he said he believed Putin when the Russian despot said he had nothing to do with the disinformation campaign identified by U.S. intelligence officials and didn't see a reason why Russia would interfere with the 2016 election.

Trump chose Putin over the findings of the CIA, NSA, FBI, the Director of National Intelligence.

What? Perspektivny? Certainly Trump never heard the term. And if he would say he never heard the term, he might well be telling the truth.

Trump got a perspektivny medal for undermining the entire U.S. intelligence community. He'll put that medal – a big one, like Stalin liked, next to the Purple Heart that he and we always wanted him to have.

And he can truthfully assert that Putin would have never invaded Ukraine under his watch.

That's because Putin was drinking U.S. and NATO intelligence from a fire hose thanks to to his perspektivny. There was a reason that Trump tore up notes, shut out translator's records and took top secret files to the gilded hell of Mar-A-Lago.

But that "genius," Putin. He identified the perspektivny, and it paid off spectacularly.

In the short term.

Russian experts say Putin, having the same malignant narcissism that defines Trump, surrounded himself with toadies and never got the information that the rebuilt military dominance he pursued over many years was not as robust as he was led to believe.

So while Russia ultimately still is evil enough, and powerful enough, to rape, torture and kill civilians, and play the desperate "we have nukes and will use them card," the ultimate success of the Russian war of aggression could well turn on the downside of that once valuable perspektivny. The Lapdog of Mar-A -Lago moved to weaken NATO, distance the U.S. from traditional Western allies, and erode the world's number one advocate for democratic governance.

Like a good lapdog.

After the poster boy for perspektiviny left office kicking, screaming and undermining democracy further by claiming election fraud, came the pragmatic and not insane President Joe Biden, who rushed to rebuild fractured alliances, lead NATO to unite and carry out a forceful economic and diplomatic isolation of Russia that could well ignite interest within Russia rid itself of Putin's incredibly cruel and senseless war. Russian oligarchs, not to mention the Russian people, do not want to go back in time and lose the benefits of membership in the civilized world.

Perspekitivny can bite you in the end.

Now Putin is looking at a united West, and a mostly united planet that sees Russia as a pariah. And will for decades to come.

Vlad, you overplayed your hand when the U.S. President was your marionette.

You tethered yourself to an idiot.

You should have known better when an idiot called you a genius.

Idiot.

MIKE LEONARD IS a NSNC past president and a NSNC 2018 Legacy Award recipient. He is a freelance writer and an adjunct lecturer at the Media School for Indiana University Bloomington. Twitter: @leonardbtown. Email: leonardbtown@gmail.com

The Dallas Morning News

TWO GUYS START A D-FW MASK FACTORY BUT CAN'T CATCH A BREAK. FORGET MADE IN TEXAS. CHINA ALWAYS WINS

BY DAVE LIEBER

Dave Lieber 🐦 ✉

Watchdog

January 22, 2021

ANYBODY KNOW someone who needs 200,000 N95 face masks? I know two guys who can hook you up, like tomorrow.

Anyone interested in helping these two guys who in less than a year built a mask factory in Fort Worth, determined to make America less dependent on China for all our protec- tive gear?

Meet John K. Bielamowicz and David Bail- largeon, owners of 9-month-old United States Mask Co. in northwest Fort Worth. They have a dream built on quaint notions of protecting Americans and strength-ening our national security.

So noble. So idealistic. So screwed.

They put their money and their heart into this. They built the equipment, bought the materials, hired the workers. They hung two large flags, U.S. and Texas, on their fac- tory walls to remind them of their mission.

Their N95 mask earned its safety certifica- tion from the feds. They even named their mask after the most famous year in Texas history. Meet the 1836 mask. Remember the Alamo.

Off to a good start, but then John and David ran into a force so powerful it threatens to shut their business down before it gets off the ground.

China.

But it's not only the Chinese' world- renowned price cutting that's giving them fits. China is getting an assist from Ameri- can buyers who prefer paying less for masks instead of boosting made in America, made in Texas, made in Dallas/Fort Worth.

These guys couldn't even catch a break in their home county. The Tarrant County purchasing department disqualified them

from bidding. It's a little fishy. The two guys say Tarrant asked for spe- cific Chinese models, which ruled them out.

County officials say it's because the local masks weren't tested by the public health department. But hey, the feds have already given the 1836 the safety seal of approval.

Remember the early days of coro- navirus when there weren't enough masks or protective gear, when

scammers took advantage, when panic set in?

America's reliance on China for medical products is a huge issue, David says. "It's why we founded the company."

"We thought there'd be a line of cus- tomers out the door. But we're being blocked at every corner. It's frustrat- ing."

Built from scratch

Picture these two putting it together.

"We lived, ate, breathed and slept everything N95," David says. "There's no guidebook, and it's not easy. The application process alone is 100 pages long."

But they did it. Their first mask was born in October. It's framed on the office wall.

Elsewhere in the building, there are another 200,000 masks in storage. "We're running a little slow because we don't have many orders," John says.

You'd think they could advertise, but they can't in a place that matters. Have you been to Google lately and searched for "buy N95 mask"?

You don't get products. You get a warning from Google: "Product availability may be limited, and we've removed results with excessive price increases."

The two guys say they are having difficulties placing online ads because hosts don't want to be associ- ated with fraud that runs wild in the mask industry.

"We've been fighting tooth and nail to get into the game," John says. "We tried so hard."

Both men spoke at the public meet- ing of the Tarrant County Commis- sioners this month to complain about the disqualification in their home county.

Representatives from the county purchasing department and health department defended their decision, saying the county hadn't tested the United States Mask product (even though the feds did).

But there was pushback from County Judge Glen Whitley and Commis- sioner Roy Brooks, who said, "I would like to see local companies get a chance... I would like to see you work with these guys."

There's also that nagging issue of price. The two guys bid $2.50 for each mask for the county's 100,000 mask order. Competitors came in below $2. The two guys say they have wiggle room.

Whitley said federal testing is good enough for him, but state law makes it difficult for governments to not accept the lowest bid.

Yeah, the two guys have some pricing issues to work out.

"We're not giving up on this," John says. "If Tarrant County doesn't buy our N95s, this country still needs them. We're going to work harder and be more patient."

"This is a huge wakeup call," David says. "Relying on China for our safe- ty, I think most people would agree, is not a smart decision."

In the meantime, know anybody that needs 200,000 life-saving masks? I can hook you up with the 1836. Re- member the Alamo.

. . .

NOTE: *This story received a half million page views. Since this was the only company that sold N-95s to individuals, the company sold out its inventory in three days. Most likely, with hundreds of thousand of masks sold, lives were saved. [Watchdog@dallasnews.com]*

Dave Lieber is the Watchdog for the Dallas Morning News. He is an award winning journalist, author and playwright. He is a past recipient of the NSNC Will Rogers Humanitarian Award. Visit: davelieber.org

EVEN WITH GROWTH, BISHOP FENWICK'S FOCUS REMAINS ON CREATING A FAMILY ATMOSPHERE

BY GINNY MCCABE

BISHOP FENWICK HIGH SCHOOL, located at 4855 state Route 122 in Franklin, has developed a reputation for academic excellence in an environment in which students are challenged to reach their potential. The curriculum, spiritual guidance and extra/co-curricular activities provide a well-rounded education that prepares Fenwick students for future successes.

"To know Bishop Fenwick High School is to know our students and graduates: young men and women of faith, knowledge and character, learning and living with purpose, and serving others as bold Christian leaders in the world," Blane M. Collison, principal/CEO of the school, says. "We are the Fenwick family. Fenwick is built with purpose. Built to learn. Built to lead. Built to love."

From its start as a small, community-based high school to its expansion to a regional high school, Bishop Fenwick has maintained its family atmosphere. The opportunities to build such family culture have changed through the years, but the values of family and community have remained, and they continue to be one of the first points of emphasis cited by students and families when they reference their decisions to attend the school. The school has second and third generations of family members who have attended; the Class of 2021 had four third-generation graduates.

"Fenwick is a community built on lifelong connections," JP Gregory, director of advancement at Fenwick, says. "That's why we commonly use the term 'Fenwick Family' to describe our school. We have 5,000-plus alumni spread all throughout the country and world. We have current students representing 30-plus ZIP codes, and we have teachers and coaches who have been committed to Fenwick for over 40 years. Our ability to offer programs inspiring our students to learn, to lead and to love propels our young men and women to thrive, creating a lifelong connection and commitment to Fenwick."

Fenwick provides a holistic education to an academically diverse population. The school offers a highly successful intervention program and a wide range of Advanced Placement and College Credit Plus courses. Fenwick provides opportunities for all students to find something they enjoy and in which they excel: career and college exploration, athletics, arts, service and STEM (science, technology, engineering, mathematics). The school's counselors operate in concert with the practicum of the American School Counselor Association. – *Cincy Magazine*

GINNY MCCABE IS A BESTSELLING AUTHOR, *an award-winning journalist, media professional, speaker & teacher. Her work can be seen in publications like Journal-News and Reuters. Her books have been published by Thomas Nelson/Harper Collins & Standard Publish-*

ing. Ginny has spent decades covering topics like news, entertainment, business, real estate, and faith-inspired themes. She serves as president on the board of Greater Cincinnati Society of Professional Journalists. Ginny was named "Best Freelance Writer" in 2018 and a Kiplinger Fellow in 2019. Connect with Ginny at www.ginnymccabe.com and on Twitter @ginnymccabe

THE PARABLE OF AN ENDLESS WAR

WHAT HAPPENS WHEN A COUNTRY THAT HAS SLEPT THROUGH A WAR SUDDENLY WAKES UP?

BY TONY NORMAN

Pittsburgh Post-Gazette Columnist
8/24/2021
tnorman@post-gazette.com

ONCE UPON A TIME, there was a country that preferred to fight its wars while it was asleep. It was a mighty country, capable of projecting its military and economic might around the world at will — but it wasn't a particularly thoughtful country.

To a sleeping country, all wars are sacrosanct and well funded as long as its citizens aren't compelled to sacrifice anything of value — like personal autonomy — to keep it going.

By contrast, the military that serves a sleeping country is always wide awake. After all, it is up to the bureaucracy that runs the war to keep the sounds of breaking things to a manageable level. The military keeps its fingers on the mute button while distributing the sleeping pills a society needs to drool on the pillow of its selective wars of occupation.

As long as there aren't forced conscriptions or daily dispatches confirming the brokenness of the citizen soldier volunteers who fight it and the futility of ever truly winning it, carnage somewhere else can go on indefinitely — sometimes for decades.

All a sleeping country demands in exchange for unlimited expenditure of treasure and other people's blood is to be insulated from the same kind of suffering on the home front experienced by its defenders abroad and the enemy who is never a match for its citizen soldiers on the battlefield.

It will even elect confirmed idiots to govern it while it sleeps as long as that leader agrees to never wake it during wartime with calls of sacrifice or moral accountability.

Because the enemy is always a barbarian of some sort, it is important to keep the wars asymmetric and to the sleeping country's advantage with aerial bombings, missiles, drones and easily rationalized human rights violations.

Under no circumstances is the country's sleep to be interrupted by the discordant sights and sounds of the war's brutal realities. The barbarians who dare to insult the sleeping country can't be allowed to interrupt the country's well-earned sleep as it dreams of the good, rational and morally uplifting war it is fighting abroad.

A sleeping country's dreams always confirm it is only interested in fighting the wars earlier generations fought and died for when war wasn't such a shadowy, unaccountable thing.

A country that sleeps through its wars is a country that has learned from experience that even so-called good wars are abattoirs of horror when fought fully awake. Good citizens prefer their horror stuffed into entertainment, not served arbitrarily by reality.

To avoid collective PTSD, it is better for a society that prefers sleeping through war to limit the trauma of that war to individual soldiers whose patriotism and sense of economic vulnerability compelled them to enter a living nightmare in the first place. War can never be a shared experience.

A sleeping country prefers to fight its wars on a comfortable, adjustable mattress tucked under a weighted blanket, though it knows its dreams will be interrupted by occasional bouts of insomnia and moral reckoning.

A war fought with eyes wide open results in fitful sleep at best, but a sleeping country knows tossing and turning through the night is for lesser nations. Countries with unlimited military budgets and an incurious citizenry have learned to sleep through its moral qualms like newborn babes. The weight of conscience is left to colicky nations that devote most of their annual spending to the social welfare programs for their people.

Yes, there will be a nightmare or two featuring the torture of civilians or enemy combatants. Missiles will level hospitals, and there will be drone attacks on rural wedding parties that somehow always look suspicious in the noonday sun — but as long as a country can keep a sleeping pill and a full glass of water at its bedside, all will be well!

Recently, after two decades dreaming of endless consumption and copulations, a sleeping country was abruptly shaken awake by a housekeeper who was no longer willing to honor the "do not disturb" sign the snoring country hung on the door a long time ago.

Through sleep-encrusted eyes, the country looked around its once-darkened bedroom and was immediately horrified by what it saw. Light streamed through broken blinds and ripped curtains as sounds of conflicts began slowly echoing through the room unbidden and unrepressed by sleep.

To its horror and embarrassment, the once-sleeping country suddenly realized it was also laying on a bed stinking of urine and vomit compounded by decades of neglect. It was also naked and covered with the bed bugs of moral complacency. The housekeeper did not avert its eyes.

Frantically, the once-sleeping country looked around the room and noticed that there were telltale signs that orgies of unspeakable violence had passed through at one point. Though there was blood on the walls and the distinct smell of excrement and moral compromise in the air, there were no actual bodies on the floor. The once-sleeping country breathed a sigh of relief.

The once-sleeping country threw on its underwear, still soiled from years of wallowing in its own filth. It hurriedly pulled up its pants. The housekeeper turned on the TV. The images of the aftermath of the war flooded the screen on every channel.

As the once-sleeping country searched the bedroom floor for its shirt, its shoes and its wallet, an army of cable news Scheherazades unspooled endless tales of national humiliation.

Policy analysts who had been instrumental in starting the war in the first place brazenly criticized the way the war was ending by insisting that all chaos is manageable if the retreat from an endless war is conducted by someone who is just a little more competent than the current leader. A sleeping country can declare victory even in defeat if it spends a little more time fretting over how to manage the optics and logistics of failure. The irony-deficient Scheherazades agreed.

"What about the translators who endangered their own families by helping our soldiers during the occupation of their country? Where's our loyalty?" the national storytellers shout from broadcast studios thousands of miles removed from a war they stopped reporting on regularly decades ago.

The anchors and war correspondents trade stories about the crushed aspirations of the women and girls left behind as the barbarians swept in. Even though the original reasons for embarking on the war are no longer relevant, some hint they wouldn't mind seeing it continue indefinitely so that the world understands that a sleeping country doesn't "cut and run" like its less exceptional peers.

These storytellers, many of whom came to prominence when the war started, ask how wounded veterans and limbless soldiers who made it out alive are supposed to feel knowing that decades in a country that resisted all previous foreign occupations with a ferocity that earned it the nickname "Graveyard of Empires" wasn't enough to get the job done.

"Why weren't contingency plans in place that would've assured a more orderly wakeup from a war for a country that had spent so many decades sleeping?" they hiss with righteous indignation befitting a chattering class.

"It's a crisis of competence," partisans screech, as though every previous second of the decades leading up to that moment weren't also saturated with brutal evidence of institutional and military incompetence.

Blinking back tears, the once-sleeping country wonders who it can blame for its latest humiliation. "Why did you wake me?" it asks the housekeeper. "I was sleeping the sleep of the just and dreaming of the perfect war. How dare you wake me so abruptly? Now I feel guilty about abandoning our allies."

Gazing in its direction without pity, the housekeeper handed the despondent country a bill. It was north of $2 trillion. It includes a death count of 66,999 soldiers of the foreign military it created and supported and nearly 50,000 civilians killed. Hundreds of billions will have to be spent on its own soldiers as they cycle through veteran services in the coming decades.

Meanwhile, the occupied country's ruling class fled with hundreds of millions, if not billions, skimmed from decades of military and economic aid — but that's what entitled rich people do, so no biggie. Of course, hundreds of billions will have to be spent in the coming decades to resettle 2.5 million refugees who have already fled the war a once-sleeping country slept through.

"Awake, sleepwalker," the housekeeper said with a discernible accent. "No matter how many sleeping pills you managed to gobble down over the last 20 years, the war outside was inescapable. Chaos has a way of seeping through the cracks of every war. It manifests itself even in your sleep."

"Our conscience is clear," the once-sleeping country replied. "We went to war to exact revenge on terrorists and to make the world safe for democracy. We also felt sorry for brutalized women and girls, so we continued the occupation for that country's own good."

The housekeeper laughed. "You should save your delusions for the next war. Now, please pay your debt and get out. It will take 100 years to scrub the stink of your hypocrisy out of the carpet."

. . .

--

Tony Norman
Columnist, Pittsburgh Post-Gazette
President of the National Society of Newspaper Columnists (NSNC) 2020-2022.
Advisory Board of International Consortium of Investigative Journalists (ICIJ)
Founding Board Member of International Free Expression Project (IFEP)
Partner in the National A.W. Mellon Democratic Futures Project
Member of the Pittsburgh Black Media Federation
Advisory board of Postindustrial.com
Twitter @Tony_NormanPG.
tnorman@post-gazette.com 412-263-1631.

YOUR LOCAL NEWS SOURCE IS DYING.
WHAT ARE WE GOING TO DO ABOUT IT?

BY CHRISTOPHER SIX

Christopher Six, Freelance Journalist, Columnist,
Legacy and New Media Marketing Professional.
301.473.6618
301.500.0410
chrissix@gmail.com
cdsix.com
Occasional Musings

DO I HAVE YOUR ATTENTION? Once upon a time, when people browsed through a newspaper page by page, headlines were designed to catch the eye. To convey a taste of what the article was about and draw you in and read the full story.

In today's world of feeds and apps, headlines may be the only blurb a reader takes away. So I didn't bury the lede. I gave you the whole thing at the top.

Your local news source is not in good shape. It is dying.

What makes me say this?

I read a fascinating article the other day by Kevin Frazier, editor of The Oregon Way, a nonpartisan online publication. The article appeared in The American Conservative magazine under the title "Local news is collapsing" and made the case that one of the political parties should take on the cause.

He makes the same points many of us who are local news advocates make — local news is a cornerstone of democracy, bolsters small business and champions the community — all hills both dominant political parties say they would make a stand on.

Indeed, Congress has shown interest, typically spurred on whenever a hedge fund gobbles up another newspaper group. The Local Journalism Sustainability Act, initially introduced in the House in July 2020 with bipartisan support died, in the Ways and Means Committee. That bill has been reintroduced in the wake of the purchase of Tribune Publishing by hedge fund Alden Global Capital.

That's great. But I, for one, don't put much faith in Congress swooping in on its white steed to save the day. Congress doesn't move that quickly. And too often, partisans seem more interested in exploiting the appetite for local news to advance their own agendas.

In the real world, community journalism faces an immediate problem. That was highlighted in the Frazier article, citing numbers that appear to have come from a Pew Research Center study released in 2019.

71% of those surveyed believed their local news outlets were doing a good job.

66% felt they were doing a good job keeping an eye on political leaders

62% thought they dealt fairly with all sides

That's encouraging. In an increasingly polarized climate, most surveyed felt their local news sources were doing a pretty good job of avoiding the biases of those on the national level.

However, here are a couple of sobering numbers:

71% of those surveyed believed local media was in good shape financially

Only 14% said they had paid for local news in the past year.

Even for someone who has been harping for as long as I have about the state of the business, these numbers are striking.

Just to reiterate what I have cited in the past, according to research by The Center for Innovation and Sustainability in Local Media, an initiative of the UNC Hussman School of Journalism and Media, nearly one-quarter of the local newspapers in existence in 2004 are gone. Many places that have no source for local news are referred to as "news deserts."

Often, newspapers that do remain are "ghosts" — filled with submitted and syndicated copy — due to aggressive cost-cutting, including dramatically slashing staff and selling off real estate. Many such properties are owned and/or operated by hedge funds and private equity funds. And, as the Tribune sale proves, that number is still growing. The New York Times did a fine piece a year ago on a colleague of mine who finds himself in that very situation.

Additionally, the pandemic has caused further newsroom layoffs, furloughs and closures nationwide. The Poynter Institute has been tracking those numbers, an exhaustive list most recently updated July 13.

Those reporters and editors who remain have been sounding the alarm on their Op-Ed pages for years. Even simply picking up a newspaper, if one is still available in your area, would likely prove it to be a shadow of its former self. Quite possibly even identical to the one next to it from a neighboring community, save the different nameplate, due to joint ownership.

But if only 14% have actually paid for news in the last year, those reporters and editors are preaching to the choir. How else to account for that 71% who believe local media is in good shape? They likely based that judgment on an assumption.

A personal example. When a particularly robust, family-owned newspaper where I grew up was bought out by a hedge fund, I had a number of friends ask me, "what happened to my newspaper?" I could only reply that I had been warning them for years, but no one was listening.

You don't know what you don't know, and certainly don't know what you got till it's gone. It wasn't on their radar until they picked up the paper and saw what had happened. Too many other things were screaming for their attention.

For the first time, I feel safe in the prediction that small community local newspapers — the legacy titles — are finished.

For one thing, most of these companies have slashed human resources and infrastructure, two of the three "big ticket" items. The third is the print costs. That means going to a completely online model (website or app) is next.

At first glance, that makes sense. One of the things that strikes me about the 14% number is that it confirms an unsurprising behavioral change. People don't have time to read the paper. They no longer need to rely on it for calendars, classifieds and pictures of their kids in the community. Papers stack up until they are tossed until eventually the consumer figures out a subscription isn't cost-effective.

The news-consuming audience has fundamentally changed. Lives are too busy and complicated to take time to peruse a newspaper. It is far easier to get a notification on technology, see something in a social media feed based on an algorithm or read something shared by a friend. No matter how flawed that method may be, it has become the simplest way to consume local news.

Unfortunately, most local newspapers have not created an online business model that supports that kind of behavior. Local sites either have to support themselves through advertising or charging readers.

Web advertising is a different beast to print advertising, and too few newspapers have adjusted their rates to compensate for that shift. Paywalls make sense for The New York Times, Washington Post and Wall Street Journal because of the demand for their exclusive kind of content. In my experience, on the local level, readers seem resigned to finding ways around a paywall or simply give up when they hit it.

So, what's next? Some organizations have turned to nonprofit models. Others have pressed for subsidizing news. The jury is still out on the sustainability of such courses.

Subsidies, in particular, give me pause. While I agree wholeheartedly in the importance of local news, I have never viewed it as a public service. Rather, I see it as a product to be sold to a consumer. If you can't sell it, in my mind you need to figure out why and repackage it into something sellable. After all, if you are subsidizing an unsellable product, you are simply passing along the cost to the same public that doesn't want what you are selling in the first place.

I admit those are personal hang-ups, I'm a capitalist at heart, but I think local news is a sellable product. Those numbers cited that said a healthy majority believed their local news outlets were doing a good job, kept an eye on their political leaders and dealt fairly with all sides should be seen as signs of encouragement.

As I have often said in this space, local news will survive in some fashion, if not in the way we know it now. There is a demand for it and nature abhors a vacuum. Ben Smith, media columnist for The New York Times, highlighted a few ventures in his most recent column. Some were issues-oriented organizations, but some straight out benefit local news and local newsgathering operations.

I recently was fortunate to work in a consulting role with a news site tied to a local radio station. It combines the resources and reach of the station to benefit its online "newspaper," helping fill the gap in one of these "news deserts." A 24/7 news operation as opposed to a weekly print product. I think that model holds promise.

The future of local news is going to take such innovation. Most legacy news outlets on the local level are too tied to old ways and technologies or lack the motivation or know-how to make this transition. Indeed, in many communities, it is too late. Those newspapers have ceased to be.

As I see it, it's going to take three ingredients to seek each other out for community journalism to reinvent itself:

People in the community who demand coverage and accountability

Professionals trained in credible newsgathering and how to produce it

Those who have the resources to make it happen

So, the question is, how badly do we want it? I'm game. How about you?

EMAIL CHRISTOPHER SIX: chrissix@gmail.com

THE UNLOVED DIAMOND RING: POSSESSIONS OF THOSE PASSED

BY SUZETTE MARTINEZ STANDRING

The Patriot Ledger
10/13/2021

HALLOWEEN, All Souls Day and The Day of the Dead are reminders of loved ones now passed. We treasure what they left behind, like a favorite piece of jewelry. Or was it? My mother's engagement ring has quite a story, and now at age 67, I understand why she never wore it.

She married my dad in 1950, and later in the 1980's, after my mother's death, the sparkly European-cut diamond ring was appraised at $5,000. How did my father afford it back when he was a steward in the U.S. Navy? Growing up in a poor neighborhood in San Francisco, I assumed my mother never wore it for fear of getting robbed or losing it. As a young girl, I said, "Mom, why don't you ever wear it? It's so beautiful!"

She said nothing. It had a very different value for her. It was her financial safety net. My mother would pawn it for money to get our family through to the end of the month, and she always bought the ring back.

This is her ring's origin story: My father, while serving in the Navy, won the diamond ring from a shipmate while gambling.

Now I am an older woman and I intuit why my mother never wore it. Some sailor spent a fortune on a ring destined for his own sweetheart. I imagine his sadness following my father's win. An engagement ring that was never chosen with my mother in mind. A ring that made my father lucky probably felt unlucky to her.

So when the ring became mine, I thought only of a disappointed fiancee somewhere in the world decades ago. My association with it was when I went with my mom to the pawn shop.

Yet it is a magnificent ring, and its history hearkens back to when my mother's original name was Josefa, later Americanized to "Josie." The only piece of real jewelry she ever owned.

When my daughter Star had her first child, I gave her the ring to mark the momentous occasion. For years, Star wore it along with her own wedding set, and felt it was as unique as her "Lola" (Filipino for grandmother).

Star said, "It's a style that you can't find today and it has an exciting acquisition story. It makes me feel pretty and special and it is my tie to Lola. When I look at it, I feel happy. It lightens my mood."

Feelings that perhaps my mother didn't have, but now new energy and meaning imprint the ring, infused with my daughter's happy memories and associations.

Do you think items retain the energy of their owners? I do.

I said, "Wear it on All Souls Day. It will guide Lola to come visit you."

Star said, "I thought the same thing!"

We've come a long way. Somewhere in the spirit world, my mom knows that it all ended very well.

EMAIL SUZETTE STANDRING: *suzmar@comcast.net or visit www. readsuzette.com*

A MATTER OF LIFE, DEATH AND FAITH: COMING TO GRIPS WITH THE INEVITABLE

BY BILL TAMMEUS

Published February 27th, 2022
https://www.flatlandkc.org

DEATH, which many Americans seem to think is optional, has been my close companion for two years. It's driven me and many others to our knees, in both despondency and prayer.

Death — through COVID-19 and such spinoff calamities as mental health breakdowns and economic disasters, plus violence in our streets and now slaughter in Ukraine — often has stolen our confidence, our hope.

We've seen it in so many places.

People have died in nursing homes while family members, barred from the room, have stood outside watching helplessly through a window.

Funerals, which might have comforted the grieving, have been postponed, then postponed again. Some may never happen.

Health care workers, clergy, first responders, funeral directors, teachers and others have been sucked into death's intense vortex, some of them permanently damaged by the collapse of their mental or physical health or both. I know pastors who pray for strength to manage just one more day.

Students often have been out of school, learning instead (sort of) virtually and falling behind as they fear that dreams of a gleaming future have died aborning.

Teenagers at summer camps, in scouting and in other group activities — strained by forces they have little capacity to understand or control — have acted out in distressing ways, requiring counselors to use techniques they hope don't make things worse. When worse happens anyway, it sometimes means suicide.

Rep. Jamie Raskin (D-Maryland) wrote about exactly that in his new book, "Unthinkable: Trauma, Truth and the Trials of American Democracy," in which he describes the suicide of his son, who was buried the day before the Jan. 6, 2021, insurrection in Washington: "I did not want to further darken his mood. But there was no way I could steer him clear of the barrage of news images of the COVID-19 body count, the corpses piling up outside hospitals, the suffering of children losing parents and the anguish of parents losing children ..."

Add to that the death in public places. Names of the dead now are chanted against racism, police brutality, inhumanity: George Floyd, Duante Wright, Breonna Taylor, Ahmaud Arbery, Cameron Lamb, so many more. Kansas City recorded 179 homicides in 2020 and 157 in 2021, while 2022 also has started out murderous. There's been blood everywhere — here, at our nation's Capitol, in Afghanistan, on and on.

Many of us also know people dying from something besides COVID, but their struggle seems more poignant now. Cancer, for instance, has almost killed a childhood friend of mine — a man of much grace. Recently on Facebook he posted a list of books he's read "in researching how to prepare for my own death." At the end of 2021, he wrote: "I'm happy. This may sound crazy or impossible coming from a dying man, but it's true." Then he listed many reasons. What a model he is.

And while we're dealing with all this and more, our shattered, polarized politics has pummeled us in incalculable ways, even as death sometimes has forced a personal reckoning about the nature and purpose of life, raising ancient questions about evil, suffering, God.

Recently, a self-described atheist wrote this in a piece for New York

Magazine: "I thought several hundred times this year, Maybe I should go to church."

Religion is being tested brutally now. Does it have anything useful to say about death, angst, uncertainty, grief? Is it a source of hope for us? Or have we been abandoned on a wounded planet crowded with people making destructive, self-centered decisions to poison the globe, oppress their neighbors and fight to keep whatever advantages they have?

I come at these tortuous questions as a Christian. As my friend Fr. W. Paul Jones writes in his new book, "Remnant Christianity," he has wagered on the Christ event (as have I), choosing to live as if it's true because he wants it to be true and because he believes it is true.

We both reject a faithless alternative. As Paul writes: "While evil is the enigma for believers, beauty is the enigma for the unbeliever. While death defies the Christian, a mockingbird defies the atheist — while both expose the agnostic as lacking in courage to struggle with life at its deepest level."

That — wrestling with life's mysteries, especially in this prolonged winter of our discontent — is what we're called to do. Not because we are — or are not — people of faith, but because we're human. It's our job. That's why I find it so discouraging when people waste the gift of time on circuses, which is to say on shallow, even addictive entertainments.

Several years ago, a book took on part of that question: "Entertaining Ourselves to Death: The Crisis in Christian Youth Culture," by Andrew Strom. It was aimed at the practice of having to amuse kids in church just to get them engaged in questions of faith.

But it's not just young people who at times seem to want to be entertained to death. It's also many adults. I'm not talking here about necessary recreation and restorative game playing. I'm talking, rather, about mindless activities (or inactivities in front of hypnotic electronic screens) that keep us from engaging the questions raised by our two years of death's menacing growl.

I've spent lots of this time walking in cemeteries. It reminds me of where I'm headed. It makes me wonder how people under the headstones spent their lives. It forces me to think again about what I want people to remember about my own presence on this planet. And it confronts me with hard questions. Whom have I hurt? Did I use my gifts and talents for others? What drove me? How could a god of infinite wisdom and creativity possibly care about me?

We're not yet done with this intense time of death. But while it's still here I don't want to use it to escape the human condition, but to celebrate it. I choose not to focus on the evil, the ugliness, the disasters that inevitably are part of life, but on the beauty, the wonder, the miracles.

Exactly that happened at a recent funeral I attended for an Episcopal priest who had developed a deep connection to — and love of — Hawaii. Everyone got a flower lei to wear and lots of people wore bright Hawaiian shirts.

It was a cool way of doing what we all should do: Tell old Mr. Death he won't have the last word.

BILL TAMMEUS, *an award-winning columnist formerly with The Kansas City Star, writes the "Faith Matters" blog for The Star's website and columns for The Presbyterian Outlook and formerly for The National Catholic Reporter. His latest book is "Love, Loss and Endurance: A 9/11 Story of Resilience and Hope in an Age of Anxiety." Email him at wtammeus@gmail.com.*

EQUALITY – OR EQUITY? WHAT IS OUR TESTIMONY?

BY BEVERLY G. WARD

Published on February 5, 2021
https://seymquakers.org/blog/2021/02/05/equality-or-equity-what-is-our-testimony/
fsearthcare@seymquakers.org

I'VE BEEN SITTING for some time with Quakers' or Friends' testimony on Equality. And, have had a rather public discussion with Friend Hal Weaver on how our testimonies can speak to justice. The discussion and the following quote from Friend Hal's book suggest that he too has been sitting with the testimonies for some time.

Our equality testimony flows inevitably from our belief that there is that of God in every person. If we believe in Equality, we must work for Justice. British Friends remind us: 'Are you alert to the practices throughout the world which discriminate against people on the basis of who or what they are, or because of their beliefs? Bear witness to the humanity of all people, including those who break society's conventions or its laws. Try to discern new growing points in social and economic life. Seek to understand the causes of injustice, social unrest, and fear. Are you working to bring about a just and compassionate society which allows everyone to develop their capacities and fosters the desire to serve?' Facing Unbearable Truths, Harold D. Weaver, 2008

In a 2019 discussion, Friend Hal pointed out that Friends' testimonies do not address justice. I agreed and added that I had suggested that perhaps Friends needed a testimony on Equity. By now, most of us have seen some version of the graphic with three children of different heights trying to see over a fence. In one panel, each child is given the same size box stand on. That's equality. In another panel, each child is given as many boxes as needed to see over of the fence. That's equity.

Though the graphics may seem simple, they are quite powerful in explaining the difference between equality and equity. Equality begins with the assumption of sameness, "equal footing", a "level playing field", and so on. Equity begins with listening to each condition.

...the testimony of equality in some ways really might get renamed the testimony of equity because in point of fact what is the same for one person, it may not be the right solution or action for another person. So our deep commitment to seeing the divine in every person leads us to seek the right solution or right arrangement that honors each person's truth...Tom Hoopes, Amesbury Quakers, "Equality or Equity? The Quaker Testimony

Perhaps, a more equitable world will help us realize a more a just world. We can try!

BOARD OF DIRECTORS, 2021-2022

President Tony Norman
Vice President Lori Duff
Secretary Telly Halkias
Treasurer Suzette Martinez Standring
Membership Chair, Luis Martinez Fernandez
Archivist, Dave Astor
Education Chair, Mike Leonard
2021-2022 Contest Chair, Jamie Fisher
Immediate Past President, Chris Carosa
Interim Executive Director, Adam Earnheardt
Interim Social Media Director: Curtis Honeycutt
Membership Intern: Autumn Duncan

Planning Committee, 2022 Birmingham Conference

Adam Earnheardt
Lori Duff
Dr. Daniela Gitlin
Telly Halkias
Ginny McCabe

Christopher Six
Suzette Martinez Standring

DRAFT 2 DIGITAL®

DRAFT2DIGITAL—TAKE CONTROL OF YOUR PUBLISHING CAREER

D2D REMOVES the friction from writing and publishing, and empowers you to get your writing in front of the readers who want it most—for free. Find out more here: http://d2d.tips/conference

www.ingramcontent.com/pod-product-compliance
Lightning Source LLC
Chambersburg PA
CBHW070005180726
48002CB00019B/2262